# Where We Find Ourselves

SUNY series in Modern Jewish Literature and Culture
Sarah Blacher Cohen, editor

*may you always find friends, peace, joy and Home!*

# Where We Find Ourselves

*Jewish Women around the World Write about Home*

Edited by
Miriam Ben-Yoseph
and
Deborah Nodler Rosen

*Deborah Nodler Rosen*

State University of New York Press
Albany, New York

Cover image: Füstös, "Sunroom" (watercolor). Courtesy of Miriam Ben-Yoseph (private collection).

Published by State University of New York Press, Albany

© 2009 State University of New York

All rights reserved

Printed in the United States of America

No part of this book may be used or reproduced in any manner whatsoever without written permission. No part of this book may be stored in a retrieval system or transmitted in any form or by any means including electronic, electrostatic, magnetic tape, mechanical, photocopying, recording, or otherwise without the prior permission in writing of the publisher.

Excelsior Editions is an imprint of State University of New York Press

For information, contact State University of New York Press, Albany, NY
www.sunypress.edu.

Production by Eileen Meehan
Marketing by Fran Keneston

### Library of Congress Cataloging-in-Publication Data

Where we find ourselves : Jewish women around the world write about home / edited by Miriam Ben-Yoseph and Deborah Nodler Rosen.
   p. cm. — (SUNY series in modern Jewish literature and culture)
ISBN 978-1-4384-2521-4 (hardcover : alk. paper)
ISBN 978-1-4384-2522-1 (pbk. : alk. paper)
   1. Jewish women.   2. Jewish families.   3. Home.   4. Home—Psychological aspects.   5. Home—Social aspects.   I. Ben-Yoseph, Miriam. II. Rosen, Deborah Nodler.

HQ1172.W44 2009
305.48'8924—dc22                                                             2009000892

10 9 8 7 6 5 4 3 2 1

# Contents

| | |
|---|---|
| PREFACE<br>*Miriam Ben-Yoseph and Deborah Nodler Rosen* | ix |
| ACKNOWLEDGMENTS | xiii |
| INTRODUCTION<br>*Miriam Ben-Yoseph and Deborah Nodler Rosen* | 1 |
| I. DISPLACEMENT AND EXILE | 7 |
| IsraIsland<br>*Nava Semel, translated by Anthony Berris (Israel/USA)* | 9 |
| A Home Called Exile<br>*Diana Anhalt (Mexico)* | 17 |
| The Kitchen<br>*Miriam Ben-Yoseph (Romania/Israel/USA)* | 21 |
| Mirka and I (excerpt from an autobiographical novel, *The Edge of the Field*)<br>*Helen Degen Cohen/Halina Degenfisz (Poland/Belarus/USA)* | 25 |
| Independence Park: A Fiction<br>*Dina Elenbogen (USA/Israel)* | 35 |
| Burning in Cuba<br>*Jyl Lynn Felman (USA/Israel/Cuba)* | 43 |
| Homeland Security<br>*S. E. Gilman (USA)* | 57 |

A Letter to My Grandmother on Coming Home from Europe    61
*Sara Paretsky (USA)*

Marked by Carnival    67
*Dina Rubina, translated by Daniel M. Jaffe (Russia/Israel)*

Homesick    81
*Else Lasker-Schüler, translated by Janine Canan (Germany/Israel)*

Memories of My Chinese Home    83
*Eve Perkal (Poland/China/USA)*

## II. PLACE AND MEMORY    89

To Return to One's Homeland    91
*Marjorie Agosin, translated by Betty Jean Craige (Chile/USA)*

Snow Unites Jerusalem    95
*Dalia Kaveh, translated by Linda Stern Zisquit (Israel)*

From Cairo to Chicago    97
*Marcelle Levy (Egypt/USA)*

Bella, 1908    101
*Ada Molinoff (USA)*

Sisters    105
*Caroline Smadja (Tunisia/France/Israel/USA)*

Jewish Oil Brat    113
Shalom Bayit    115
*Davi Walders (USA)*

All But My Life    117
*Gerda Weissmann Klein (Poland/USA)*

Kentucky Fried Chicken    119
*Arlene Zide (USA)*

America    125
*Viva Hammer (Australia/USA)*

East     131
*Rochelle Mass (Canada/Israel)*

The Mah-Jongg Set     133
*Deborah Nodler Rosen (USA)*

A Jewish Romanian in Oxford     137
*Maria Roth (Romania)*

In the Margin     151
*Madeline Tiger (USA)*

To the Smell of Sea and Pickle     153
*Dalia Kaveh, translated by Linda Stern Zisquit (Israel)*

Isibaya (The Home)     155
*Cha Johnston (South Africa)*

## III. LANGUAGE AND CREATIVITY     159

Yiddishland     161
*Ellen Cassedy (USA)*

Silence     169
*Dalia Kaveh, translated by Linda Stern Zisquit (Israel)*

The Girl in the Balcony     171
*Angelina Muñiz-Huberman (Mexico)*

The Music and Language of Home     175
*Sara Schwarzbaum (Argentina/USA)*

Here     181
*Judith Ilson Taylor (USA)*

Posit     183
Morning Exercise     185
Renaissance     187
Line of Defense     189
*Linda Stern Zisquit (USA/Israel)*

## IV. FAMILY AND TRADITION ... 191

I, May I Find Home ... 193
*Dorothy Field (USA)*

The Dina Letters ... 195
*Barbara F. Lefcowitz (USA)*

My Indian Bene Israel Home ... 201
*Erusha Newman (India/USA)*

In Your Letter ... 207
*Julie Parson-Nesbitt (USA)*

If Only I'd Been Born a Kosher Chicken ... 209
*Jyl Lynn Felman (USA/Israel/Cuba)*

My Mother's Roots ... 221
*Helen Degen Cohen/Halina Degenfisz (Poland/Belarus/USA)*

My Iranian Sukkah ... 225
*Farideh Dayanim Goldin (Iran/USA)*

Home for Thanksgiving ... 235
*Rachel Goldin Jinich (USA)*

At Home in Shabbat ... 239
*Arlene Hisiger (USA/Israel)*

Learning the Language ... 243
*Tracy Koretsky (USA)*

When We Are Born We Are Given a Golden Tent and
All of Life Is the Folding and Setting Up of the Tent ... 253
*Edith Altman (Germany/USA)*

## NOTES ON CONTRIBUTORS ... 257

# Preface

The idea of *bashert* (that events are preordained) is a much beloved one in Jewish tradition; many see it as an imaginative, intuitive force that brings together people and the projects they most desire. It was *bashert* that Miriam Ben-Yoseph, originally from Romania, and Deborah Nodler Rosen, whose grandparents emigrated from Romania, would meet, become friends, and together turn Miriam's dream of this anthology into reality.

Ben-Yoseph experienced exile and homelessness in the country of her birth (Romania), then in her moves to Israel, and finally to the United States. Her interest in the subject of home derives mainly from her personal experience and from her search for what it means to be at home in the world. Increasingly, the concept of home has come to define her work as well. Her teaching, research, and writing often focus on themes related to home.

Rosen lives her life in search mode, seeking connections to the Jews of the world because she is certain that if her roots are traced back far enough a few will lead through India, Iraq, and China to Jerusalem. Therefore, it was *bashert* that at an Association of Writers & Writing Programs convention attended by 4,000 writers, Rosen would meet the writer from India whose Jewish family is part of the ancient Bene Israel community of Jews in Bombay. And that in a four-seater ferry on China's Yellow River, her fellow passengers would be Iraqi Jews who lived in India and now reside in Canada.

*Where We Find Ourselves: Jewish Women around the World Write about Home* captures women's many-faceted yearnings for home.

We want to thank our editorial board composed of Helen Degen Cohen, Lisa Comforty, Dina Elenbogen, and Judith Ilson Taylor, whose diverse backgrounds and strong interest in the concept of home enlarged the scope of this anthology:

The lonely *state of unbelonging* (a kind of home) has influenced Helen Degen Cohen's early and adult life. A Holocaust survivor who spent time in a ghetto, in hiding, and in a Displaced Person's Camp, she has produced a body of work on what she calls not a theme but a *place*—the War ("the War gave birth to me")—perhaps one version of *the state of unbelonging* to which, ironically, she felt she did belong—the other being writing. Most of her major awards are for what came alive while in this latter *state of unbelonging*.

Lisa Comforty's abiding interest in the concept of home arises from her documentation of the rescue of Bulgarian Jewry from the Holocaust. She draws also on her life in Israel, her roots in the lost world of Jewish Poland, and the transplanted world of Jewish Chicago.

Dina Elenbogen wrestled with the idea of home as she traveled back and forth between America, the land where she was born, and Israel, the country that has felt most like home to her. Her questions about home found expression in her poetry, essays, stories, as well as in her recently completed book-length memoir about her work helping to absorb Ethiopian Jews into Israeli society. In her memoir Elenbogen asks: Has Israel truly become home to the Ethiopian Jews, and can Israel be home to her, an American Jewish woman and poet?

For as long as Judith Ilson Taylor can remember, the creative drive has been a powerful force in her. As an artist, teacher, and writer, she continually explores ways to express it. In her questions and in the work that emerges from them, in the process and in all its many landscapes is where she finds herself and makes her home.

In addition, we want to thank Marjorie Agosin, the Luella Lamer Slaner Professor of Latin American studies at Wellesley College, who put us in touch with many Latin American authors.

*Where We Find Ourselves: Jewish Women around the World Write about Home* speaks in the voices of forty Jewish women who in turn represent the voices of Jewish women around the world and throughout history, telling us what we have forgotten or never knew about being at home in the world. We are grateful to them.

# Acknowledgments

Edith Altman, "When We Are Born We Are Given a Golden Tent and All of Life Is the Folding and Setting Up of the Tent," previously published in *Edith Altman: Retrospective* (Altenburg, Germany: Lindenau-Museum, 2003), pp. 112–117. Reprinted by permission of the author.

Miriam Ben-Yoseph, "The Kitchen," published in an earlier version in *Emergence IV: Fiction and Poetry by Emerging Women Writers* (Bridgeview, IL: Emergence Publishing Company, 1998), pp. 43–47. Reprinted by permission of the author.

Ellen Cassedy, "Yiddishland," previously published as "Home, In So Many Words" in *Hadassah Magazine* 88:5 (2007), and in *Homelands: Women's Journeys Across Race, Place, and Time* edited by Patricia Justine Tumang and Jenesha de Rivera (Emeryville, CA: Seal Press, 2006). Copyright © 2006, 2007 by Ellen Cassedy. Reprinted by permission of the author.

Jyl Lynn Felman, "If Only I'd Been Born a Kosher Chicken," previously published in *Tikkun Magazine* 9:4 (July/August 1994), pp. 47–50. Reprinted by permission of the author.

Dorothy Field, "I, May I Find Home," excerpted from *Leaving the Narrow Place* by Dorothy Field (Lantzville, British Columbia: Oolichan Books, 2004), p. 72. Reprinted by permission of the author and Oolichan Books.

Dalia Kaveh, "Snow Unites Jerusalem" and "To the Smell of Sea and Pickle" (translated by Linda Stern Zisquit) previously published in

*E-sha E-gool* (Tel Aviv: Hakkibutz Hameuchad Publishing House, 1990), p. 35 and 44. "Silence" (translated by Linda Stern Zisquit) previously published in *Rain* (Tel-Aviv: Hakibbutz Hameuchad Publishing House, 2001), p. 54. Reprinted by permission of the author and Hakibbutz Hameuchad Publishing House.

Else Lasker-Schüler, "Homesick," previously published in *Star in My Forehead: Selected Poems by Else Lasker-Schüler*, translated by Janine Canan (Duluth: Holy Cow Press, 2000), p. 39. Reprinted by permission of the translator.

Rochelle Mass, "East," previously published in *The Startled Land* by Rochelle Mass (Hershey, PA: Wind River Press, 2003), p. 20, and in *Jewish Women's Literary Annual* (2003), p. 18. Reprinted by permission of the author.

Sara Paretsky, "A Letter to My Grandma on Coming Home from Europe," previously published in a shorter version as "Grannie, Look What We're Doing to the Land of Freedom," in the *Guardian*, January 3, 2005. Copyright © 2004 by Sara Paretsky. Reprinted by permission of the author.

Dina Rubina, "Marked By Carnival," translated by Daniel Jaffe, previously published in *Silk Road* 1:1 (Summer 2006), p. 101. Reprinted by permission of the translator.

Sara Schwarzbaum, "The Music and Language of Home," previously published as "I Didn't Know I Would End Up Like This" in *Culture and Identity: Life Stories for Counselors and Therapists* (2005) by Anita Jones Thomas and Sara E. Schwarzbaum (Thousand Oaks, CA: Sage Publications), pp. 290–295. Reprinted by permission of the author and Sage Publications.

Nava Semel, "IsraIsland," excerpted from *IsraIsland* by Nava Semel, translated by Anthony Berris. Previously published in Hebrew as *Eesrael* (Tel Aviv: Yedioth Achronot, 2006). Reprinted (in English) by permission of the author.

Davi Walders, "Jewish Oil Brat," previously published in S. Wittig Albert, ed., *What Wildness Is This: Women Write About The Southwest* (Austin: University of Texas Press, 2007), p. 192; "Shalom

Bayit," previously published in *Judaism: A Quarterly Journal of Jewish Life and Thought* 46 (Summer 1997), p. 364. Reprinted by permission of the author.

Gerda Weissmann Klein, "All But My Life," excerpted from "Epilogue" from *All But My Life* by Gerda Weissman Klein (New York: Hill and Wang, pp. 247–249. Copyright © 1957, 1995 by Gerda Weissmann Klein. Reprinted by permission of the author and Hill and Wang, a division of Farrar, Straus and Giroux, LLC; and of Victor Gollancz, an imprint of the Orion Publishing Group.

Linda Stern Zisquit: "Posit" and "Morning Exercise," previously published in *Unopened Letters* by Linda Stern Zisquit (Riverdale-on-Hudson, NY: Sheep Meadow Press, 1996), p. 29 and 28; "Renaissance," previously published in *Ritual Bath* by Linda Stern Zisquit (Seattle: Broken Moon Press, 1993), pp. 60–61; "Line of Defense," previously published in *Bridges* 10:1 (2004). Reprinted by permission of the author.

# Introduction

The longing for home is as ancient as exile from Eden and as contemporary as the dilemma of finding home in Havana, Shanghai, or Jerusalem. History and the Holocaust have intensified the struggle of Jewish women everywhere to redefine the idea of home. The selections in this anthology reflect a variety of historical, cultural, political, and religious contexts while illuminating each author's private world. Through memoir, poetry, and fiction, forty Jewish women writers from around the world address questions such as: What is home? Is it a concrete place? Is it the place you were born and raised, or is it a place you were forced to leave because of nationalism, racism, or violence? Is home where you live now, or is it an abstract composite of memories? Is home embodied in the art you create, or in the Jewish rituals you observe? This book offers accounts of journeys of discovery and the many possible meanings of home. The authors in *Where We Find Ourselves* write about Argentina, Australia, Chile, China, Cuba, France, India, Iraq, Iran, Israel, Mexico, Romania, Russia, South Africa, and the United States. Most contributors are accomplished writers, others write because they find the topic compelling. For some, English is a second, third, or even fourth language.

The anthology has been divided into four sections: Displacement and Exile; Place and Memory; Language and Creativity; Family and Tradition.

# Displacement and Exile

Displacement and Exile create suffering and a perpetual search for home whether that displacement is caused by war, anti-Semitism, communism, or unique circumstances. Yet many find unexpected opportunities in exile.

Nava Semel raises the eternal question: Where is the true Jewish home? Can it only be Zion or is there an alternative? Diana Anhalt, a political *exilée*, claims descent "from a long line of refugees—wandering Jews—who changed their addresses more often than they changed shoes." One can feel displaced in one's own home, as Ben-Yoseph points out in her short story. Helen Degen Cohen writes about the war Ghetto, the formal Ghetto instituted by the Nazis that was home to Jews until they were sent to worse places. In the background of Dina Elenbogen's story about postpartum depression, exile, and longing for home is the larger story of Jewish and Palestinian exile. Jyl Lynn Felman meditates on a Jewish North American lesbian's "herstorical" search for home and the complications that arise when she arrives in Havana.

Estrangement is also possible in one's own country. S. E. Gilman mourns the fact that after September 11, the American government seeks to make the country safe by controlling immigration. Sara Paretsky tells her grandmother that for immigrants the welcoming beacon from the Statue of Liberty has dimmed. Dina Rubina's essay comments on the difficulties encountered when bringing cultural values and linguistic associations from one's previous home (Russia) into one's new home (Israel). Else Lasker-Schüler, a German Jew, mourns the human condition as one of intrinsic exile but out of that feeling comes a poetry shimmering with childlike magic and wonder. Eve Perkal describes a life of exile in Shanghai, but she also recognizes that this was the only place on the eve of World War II that would accept a family without papers.

## Place and Memory

Over the centuries home has evolved from country and clan, becoming progressively more portable and idiosyncratic. In the twenty-first century, the idea of home oscillates between concrete places and more abstract concepts located in memory and in individual perceptions.

For Marjorie Agosin, a quintessential citizen of the Jewish Diaspora, home is in the landscape of Chile where she grew up. Dalia Kaveh sees snow-covered Jerusalem as the home that connects her to the Palestinians who also regard Jerusalem as home and to her ancestors who lived for generations in the harsh winters of Poland and Russia. Marcelle Levy traces her family odyssey from Basra, Iraq, to Cairo, Egypt, to Chicago, USA, which for her becomes home. Ada Molinoff writes about the difficult process that immigrants experience while trying to reestablish themselves in America. Caroline Smadja, who survived several uprootings, locates home in the French villa where she spent her childhood.

Davi Walders describes the role of home in memory. She considers herself lucky to have been born in America during World War II; using her deceased mother's recipe to bake challah in her adult home evokes a tender memory of mother and child working together in the quiet moments before Shabbat. For Gerda Weissmann Klein, a Holocaust survivor, home is firmly rooted in America. She loves America "as only one who has been homeless for so long can understand." Arlene Zide's notion of home is linked to an apartment in the New York neighborhood where she and her family once lived. When she finally returns to this place she realizes that memory and reality do not coincide and that, in fact, one cannot go home again.

Viva Hammer writes that home is a metaphysical concept, a place to go when you are alone in an unfamiliar setting. Rochelle Mass believes that home faces Jerusalem, source of King David's wisdom and kaffiyehed men at roadblocks. Home for Deborah Nodler Rosen is a place where she can be her authentic self and feel free to create. After visiting England, Maria Roth realizes that home is in Romania, where she can live by her parents' values and be a Jew without speaking Hebrew or following Jewish practice. Similarly, Madeline Tiger asserts that a house without Jewish ceremonies can still be a home for a Jewish woman observing her own rituals.

Dalia Kaveh describes a Tel Aviv neighborhood with courtyard gardens as a framework for the home hidden within the soul. Cha Johnston traces the journey of her soul that leads her to identify her home as herself—a white African Jewish woman.

## Language and Creativity

Many women find home not in a physical place but in language and creativity. Their creations reflect the sum total of their history which includes their Jewish heritage. Ellen Cassedy travels to Vilnius to study Yiddish in order to connect with her forebears and therefore herself. Dalia Kaveh writes about the process of creativity that emerges when she is alone in her home surrounded by emptiness and silence. Angelina Muñiz-Huberman, a lifelong traveler and *exilée*, regards her literary creation as her true home: language and words are the construct inside which her life unfolds. Sara Schwarzbaum finds home in the music and languages that her immigrant family share. Judith Ilson Taylor lives in Jewish myth. Central to that myth is the nomadic tradition, and through her life and her work she tries to express the meaning she finds in that myth and that tradition. Linda Stern Zisquit uses her work to imagine wholeness in the fragmented experience of living in at least two places. Jewish thought and ritual as well as biblical texts are integral to her life and work.

## Family and Tradition

Family and Jewish tradition form the core of home for many women. Dorothy Field wants to knit peace, a crucial aspect of home, out of clamoring family voices. Barbara F. Lefcowitz imagines a correspondence with her great-aunt Dina who immigrated to New York City, and defines home as a place where she would feel unconditionally accepted despite her deformed spine. Erusha Newman, whose family emigrated from Iran to India to America, defines home in terms of family celebrations of the Jewish holidays. Julie Parson-Nesbitt discovers after tragedy that prayer, family, and her love for poetry helped her re-create the safety and meaning of home.

Jyl Lynn Felman wishes she had been born a kosher chicken so that there would be no separation from her mother and her people. Helen Degen Cohen evokes a second meaning for the "roots" she puts into her soup, whose steam is the spiritual mist that connects her with her mother's sad past in her shtetl. Although Iran was Farideh Dayanim Goldin's original home, now home is wherever she can re-create her Iranian Sukkah. Her daughter Rachel Goldin Jinich finds home in shared food, language, and stories. Arlene Hisiger discovers home not in bricks and mortar but in the spiritual realm of the Sabbath. Tracy Koretsky finds that Jews are a people beyond borders whose homeland is in their Jewishness. Edith Altman's study of Jewish mystical teachings informs her thinking about the creative process and serves as an inspiration for *tikkun olam*, repair of the world.

The central question of our contributors is: Where do we find home? Their answers differ because their journeys differ, but all of them have unique connections to Judaism. All these women are intent on establishing home—a place, literal or metaphorical, where they can be Jewish, establish safe havens for themselves and their families, and freely express their essential selves.

# I
# Displacement and Exile

# IsraIsland

## NAVA SEMEL

*Translated from the Hebrew by Anthony Berris*

*The State of the Jews on an Indian island near Niagara Falls almost happened. Mordechai Manuel Noah, a diplomat, playwright, and journalist had purchased Grand Island in New York State in September 1825, and established a safe haven he named Ararat. However, Noah's call to world Jewry to settle on the island was rejected and no Jews arrived. Israeli writer Nava Semel's latest novel revisits this obscure footnote in American history and travels on the axis of time between Israel of today and IsraIsland—the land of the Jews that could have been. In this excerpt, the narrative is told through the eyes of Little Dove, a young Indian woman who is the sole heiress to the island that has just been purchased by the Jews as their future home. On the night before the inauguration ceremony of Ararat, Little Dove leads the "Chief Jew" to the island to show him that he hasn't bought an empty place. She struggles to overcome the impulse to destroy him and instead to give away her homeland in a peaceful way. Nava Semel's book raises the eternal question, Where is the true Jewish home? Can it only be Zion or is there an alternative?*

I was never taught how to track Jews.

Ever since my birth under the Roaring Water you showed me, Father Raven, the signs all around. Pay attention to how the ferns are broken, girl, a white-tailed deer made its way to drink. A sprig of leaves suddenly fell onto your head, the sign of a hawk that quickly flew from the top branches of a white oak. They have gone—leaving signs behind them. The world is as it is. The world as it was.

Not the tracks of Jews. You gave no sign in any world.

What I now see is not an illusion, but a vision of what came before what came before. My tiny hand is in yours, and you bring it close to the trembling line of the riverbank, but stop me separating between land and water. Then you plunge your hand into the water, as if cutting it off, but without pain.

Our own tracks were also planted along the banks of the Niagara River on that distant day: the moccasin footprints of a man who has difficulty walking and beside them, the hopping footprints of a light-footed little girl. And as we move away from the water's edge you point at the signs of the wild flailing tail of a black bass that had leapt from the water onto the bank. Not even a fish would surrender its place without a fight, I said, and you marked the signs of white thought in me.

I asked if a spirit nestled in it when it returned to the water, and you laughed. Never again did I doubt your word. I was short on days and memory too.

I did not know how deep the sickness was in your bones. To conceal your need of help, you invented a game for us: you pretended to be a grizzly bear and I was the hunter who drew it into the opening in the ferns where the white-tailed deer had blazed a trail for us. I played in the undergrowth far from your fading voice trying to explain that human beings, palefaces and redskins alike, build a barrier between themselves and the land, defying the knowledge that one day they will be forced to return to it. Cunningly you tried to teach me the secret language in which the world speaks, but I could see nothing around me other than the magic of play, a brilliant garden in which the black bass and the white dove dance in circles, as if they had been created just for me. Only in your absence I had to probe the mysteries alone, to follow the spear that no sense can perceive. And tonight the spirits bring me unfamiliar tracks. A Jew Chief sails in a canoe carved with my own hands, with his weight slowing the journey to the island.

We sailed from Buffalo, a flourishing white man's village. In my eyes it is a temporary place, but permanent in the eyes of Mistress Lennox.

I paddle in the dark and the Jew Chief gazes toward the black horizon like a blind man seeking a familiar landscape. He arouses compassion in me. We will be there soon, I tell him. Don't you trust me?

Even if I were to extinguish my eyes the waterway would open before me, for the currents gather my canoe and bring it home. I paddle in the darkness and detect signs of fear in my passenger's silence. He hides behind his expression like the young men before their initiation rite. Yet my passenger is not a youngster but a man who has sailed many waters and crossed worlds. For six days the guest had sat in the splendid parlor at Mistress Lennox's homestead and recounted his adventures, with all of Buffalo's gentry sitting around him with gaping eyes and mouths.

On this night, the seventh since he came from New York, the gateway to the East, he is gripping the sides of my canoe as if in a cradle. Perhaps he is afraid I will deliberately drown him or maybe his tribe is not accustomed to a woman navigating.

I told him: The Great Spirit will guide us, and did not tell him, Father Raven, that your bones are resting there, waiting for their final burial, the custom of the tribe.

You are the last one, you told me. Guard our bird-shaped island embraced in the arms of Niagara.

On that far-off day you dipped my little hand into the shivering line between land and water and demanded that I swear my loyalty to "The Low Land that grows many herbs."

I paddle along the river of memory toward what came before what came before. A father sheds his feathers and guides his daughter toward the coming of visions. You asked me not to rebel against them lest I be smitten by the plague of the white man, like the other sicknesses they had brought with them from their distant places. But I was filled with terror of the uninvited scenes that invaded my spirit, and was already jealous of the palefaces for their refusal.

I am the last of the last, and I have not kept my oath to protect the island under my wing. Tomorrow it will pass to its new owners with paper money. The Jew Chief bought it from the authorities and as dawn breaks he will declare it to be the legal possession of his tribe and gather them in from the four corners of the earth.

There are other islands in the world apart from the little piece of land into the river. This is not a great sea to where fame-seeking mariners sail to discover its secrets. Yet this island is my home, the whole world for me, but what is it for the Jew Chief? Just a tiny patch drawn with a quill on the scrolls of paper the white man calls "maps." Without them they cannot take even a single step. They even wrote its name above the blot on the map in curved letters: "Grand Island." But on their scrolls there were none of the footprints sown in this place, not even the soft soil that turns yellow in summer and the canopy of foliage that whispers in the fall. The coyotes, the raccoons, the doves and the ravens, all move in circles under the maple and elm trees. Everything is in its place as if there is no Buffalo, no America, and only this island exists. And now he owns it, my enforced inheritor's promised land.

A Jew.

If it were not for me he would not even put a foot on it.

We glide into the inlet and I extend my hand to help the Jew Chief out of the rocking canoe, but he ignores it and slips between water and land. Like a wild goose he waddles a little and quickly gets up. If his feet were as small as mine I'd give him my moccasins and walk barefoot. But he is a big man and I am only Little Dove.

He didn't even ask my name when we left, but he gave me his twice: Mordecai Manuel Noah. I looked for the marks of a chief and did not find a colored feather headdress or even the pieces of metal the palefaces adorn themselves with at the end of a battle.

I say: Welcome, and he replies: In whose name do you welcome me, woman? This island is empty.

Does the Jew Chief have poor eyesight or is he deaf? How can he not sense the natives whispering in the leaves, the water and the soil? How can he lead his tribe if he is unable to see spoor, and how can I teach him the entire Book of Signs in one night?

At the end of every summer I leave Buffalo and paddle to the green Low Land. I do not know who gave the island its red name so many suns and moons ago. At the end of every summer Mistress Lennox gives me her blessing for the journey, much to the master's annoyance. He fears I will not return and my mistress will have to work in the cornfields on her own. From me she learned how to grind flour in a hollow stump, and how to beat a copper pot and then be as silent as a scarecrow to drive away the birds—so we protect the fields from interlopers with our bodies. There, in the raised shelter, overlooking the sea of young corncobs, a thread of friendship was spun between us. Last winter, when the snow drifted high and we were forced to stay indoors for many days, Mistress Lennox asked me to call her by her Christian name, but I did not dare cross that line.

She never asked me what I do on the island by myself at the end of every summer, and I did not tell her how, in my mind's eye, I go into the long house built by my ancestors, walk through the ashes and listen to the murmuring of the old ones. The Huron and Neutral and Seneca tribes flow in the currents and whirlpools, the covenant of the Iroquois Nation that guarded the gateways to East and West.

What came before what came before will not be recorded in the white man's books.

Now I steady the bow of my canoe on the shore, leaving the rest in the water. I stow the fin-smooth paddle in the bottom of the canoe and fold the reed mat that protected my knees as I paddled. The water glistening like the wampum beads embroidering my belt, and I touch it. The belt will protect me from the unknown.

The moment he arrived at the Lennox homestead the Jew Chief began waving his land deed. At first I thought he made the wind blow but he claimed that it was a valuable property, as if he had gained a rare treasure.

Mistress Lennox asked me: This is your birthplace, is it not, and did not wait for a reply.

Mistress Lennox's husband took the deed from the Jew Chief and rolled it in his fingers, the way he examines the silver pelt of a grizzly bear and haggles with the Inuit hunter who has come afar to reach us from the wilderness beyond the great falls. For a long time Mistress Lennox's husband studied the small, dense writing marks on the paper, and in the end declared: You're a lucky man, Major Noah, pulling the right strings, and then he winked, You Jews ... as if to say: You Indians.

I hazarded a red thought: Land is not property, it is given to all people for safekeeping, and the men in the parlor in Buffalo rolled their laughter around like barrels.

Mistress Lennox's husband whispered something to the Jew Chief, and then turned to me. His words, as always, were slow and measured.

Land is merchandise, girl, just like the corn you help us grow and in exchange for our protection. This is a new world. But you wouldn't understand, girl.

Again he addressed the guest:

How much did you pay, Major Noah? A real bargain. If only we'd known that Grand Island was up for sale....

Then Mistress Lennox's husband began pacing the parlor, making calculations. He had not returned the deed to the guest.

Perhaps there are other countries for sale, said Mistress Lennox, countries that can be bought cheaply because nobody wants to live or die there. A penal island, like Elba or St. Helena, to which the deposed Emperor Napoleon was exiled many suns ago.

Once more the men's laughter echoed through the parlor.

Mistress Lennox's husband suddenly tensed. His white thought paled even more and he blurted: So close to us...an island of Jews.

His hand moved toward his musket.

At that moment I said to the Jew Chief: I will take you there.

A penal island.

An island of exiles...

Jews? What are they? Who are they?

Do not Father Raven and Little Dove have the right to know who their inheritors are?

# A Home Called Exile

### Diana Anhalt

*"Once upon a time in the middle of the night a little girl was awakened by pounding on the door. 'Pogrom! Pogrom! Hide under the bed,' screamed her mother. 'Hide under the bed,' and the little girl jumped out from under her quilt and hid under her bed. She heard shouting, the stomping of boots, and the barking of dogs. After what seemed like a long time, she smelled smoke and crawled out. Her house was on fire, but she escaped her house and her village and went to America and lived happily ever after."*

"Now that is a True Life Story," said my grandmother—who tended to speak in capital letters—"about a little girl just like you." I never believed it was about a little girl just like me. (I believed it was about a little girl just like her. Although she never said so.) Nor would she tell me what had happened to the little girl, to her family, to her home.

"But how did she get to America?" I'd ask.

She wouldn't tell me that either. Instead, she'd help me change into my pajamas, feed me challah and honey at her kitchen table, and curl my hair, dampening the ends with spit, and coiling the tendrils onto a curling iron heated over the range. "Well, if you don't know," I'd say, "how do you know she lived happily ever after?"

"She lived happily ever after because when she got to America she arrived home. And home is a place where you can sleep all night without having to worry about Cossacks at the door."

After hearing such stories I occasionally dreamed I was wedged into a corner between the bed and the wall. I couldn't move, and the air was filled with the scent of burning hair. I tried to call for help, but no words came. I would awake, sweat-soaked, gasping for breath. Yet, despite my nightmares, I still looked forward to spending Friday nights on my grandmother's green velvet sofa, which smelled, as she did, of mothballs and chicken broth. She would sing about a calf bound for market—*dona dona dona dona*—and the ladybug: "... fly, fly, fly away home, your house is on fire...." There was also a song in Yiddish, which, she told me, was about a bird, a *fagele*, who abandoned her nest.

Today, I realize my grandmother's True Life Stories were prophetic: Shortly after she died—I was eight by then—I too was rudely awakened—metaphorically, at least—by 'Cossacks at the door' and forced to leave my home and my blissful life in the Bronx.

We lived in Parkchester then, and I attended PS 106. It was located in the kind of neighborhood where just about everyone, including me, learned how to roll a decent spitball long before we could read or write, but where, during the day, we could safely roam the streets—as long as we didn't try to cross without adult supervision. There was a fenced-in concrete playground where we jumped rope and drew in our hopscotch games with colored chalk. My mother tied my roller skate key around my neck with a long red ribbon, and I skated everywhere—down the long corridor to our elevator, out the door to the playground, to the grocery, even to school—when the weather allowed. There was whitefish or lox and bagels on Sunday mornings, summer picnics with my cousins at Pelham Bay Park, ice-skating in the winter, and the *Howdy Doody Show* on television every weekday afternoon.

For years I wondered: Why would anyone want to leave all this? Why, from one day to the next, would my parents turn their backs on their birthplaces, their jobs, and their families and run away from home? Perhaps, had I remembered what my grandmother used to say, I wouldn't have been so surprised: "Our Family Reunions always take place in Bus Terminals and Train Stations—Or at Funerals. We were born with Wheels on our Heels. Like Taxicabs." She knew what she was talking about. After all, we were descended from a long line of refugees—wandering Jews—who changed their addresses more often than they changed shoes. My parents merely followed in their footsteps.

Leaving behind former lives, they stepped out into new ones and expected me to do likewise. But I didn't want to. Apparently, neither did they, although, I didn't know that at the time. I thought they left the Bronx because they wanted to make my life miserable.

If my grandmother had been alive, it's possible she might have recognized the parallel between her departure from Poland during the pogroms and ours, some fifty years later, during a pogrom of another sort: Joseph McCarthy's witch hunts targeting suspected communists and fellow travelers.

The year was 1950 and, by then, the widely held perception of American Communists engaged in a worldwide conspiracy directed against their own country had begun to take hold. Amid a scenario marked by anti-Red rhetoric, restrictive legislation, loyalty oaths, and a series of highly publicized political hearings, hundreds of radicals or former radicals were running for cover.

My parents fled to Mexico. They were not alone. Other American families—by my calculations close to seventy—would come to call Mexico home for either a few weeks, a few months or—as in my parents' case—for thirty years. Because it was one of only two countries—Canada was the other—that required no passports of American citizens, it became an attractive alternative for dissidents on the run. (The State Department routinely denied travel documents to the politically suspect.)

At the beginning, home for us was wherever we managed to remain for any length of time: the apartment on Dickens Street with its paper-thin walls; the little house on *Calle* La Fontaine next door to the U.S. Embassy's Legal Attaché. (He denounced my father, and we moved for the third time to a house in the Pedregal area.)

While we had shaken Bronx's soil from our shoes, we hadn't shaken the FBI. They, often with the cooperation of the Mexican authorities, intercepted our phones, opened our mail, exposed us in the media, and dogged our footsteps. (My parents were under surveillance for eighteen years.)

Thus, understandably, we lived quiet, vigilant, somewhat uncertain lives on the edge of a society that regarded us as outsiders. Sometimes, I believed I didn't have a home—not a real one—until I left my parents' house. By then—some fifteen years after we'd left New York—the secrecy surrounding my parents' past and their self-imposed exile from the Bronx no longer cast so long a shadow. I married Mauricio, a Mexican citizen. We moved into an apartment of our own and started raising a family. During the first years of our marriage I remember thinking: *Well, finally. I belong to this place. I no longer live in exile.* But that was not completely true.

Because in the end, exile—and I use that word loosely—is simply one more characteristic of the human condition. I realized that all of us, starting with Adam and Eve, are, to one degree or another, outcasts in search of a home. When the time comes, each of us must leave our childhood homes and seek safe haven elsewhere.

Given our history, starting with the image of the "Wandering Jew" fleeing the Egyptians, the Crusaders, the Spanish Inquisitors, the Cossacks, or the Nazis—we Jews, though we hold no monopoly on human suffering—have become an icon for pain and affliction. Thus, it is understandable that, throughout the centuries, the concept of home for the Jew has been an essentially simple one: a secure place where one can subsist and light the Sabbath candles with some guarantee of privacy and respect. Or, to paraphrase my grandmother: ". . . home is a place where you can sleep all night without having to worry about Cossacks at the door."

# The Kitchen

## Miriam Ben-Yoseph

If you come to my house in Evanston, sooner or later you will spend time in my favorite room in the house, my kitchen, the room that means home to me. Still, when I think about a kitchen, it is my first kitchen that comes to mind, the kitchen of my childhood in Sighisoara, my hometown in Romania.

That kitchen was the center of our home for my family. After our house was nationalized by the communists and other families came to live with us, the kitchen became the center of their lives too. But I know that my mother and grandmother missed the days when the house had belonged only to our family. In fact, after our house was nationalized, my grandmother never again set foot in the kitchen. She preferred to stay in her room, pretending that nothing had happened—just as she did during all those years when my father was a political prisoner and she pretended to believe that he was only on an extended overseas trip. Sometimes she would wonder aloud why he was not writing to her. "I just cannot understand that," I would hear her mutter to herself. My mother and my aunt would give each other meaningful looks, doubting that Grandma really believed the overseas story. They would have conversations about my father in front of my grandmother who was a little hard of hearing, and in front of me, assuming that I was too young to understand what they were talking about. But Grandma heard and I understood.

When I did not like something I also wanted to pretend, but my mother told me I was too young, implying that to pretend was a privilege one earned with age. I couldn't accept that, so I began by practicing little deceits, and the kitchen was a great place to start.

The new families assigned by the government to move into our house thought that they had a right to share not only our kitchen but also our food. This upset my mother who preferred not to eat at all after someone stuck a hand into one of her pots or trays of food. Whenever she had to leave the kitchen, she'd asked me to stand by the stove.

"They would not dare stick their dirty hands into our food while the child is there," I heard her say to her friend Margareta, the judge's wife from across the street.

But frequently they did dare, dipping into everything or anything they thought they might like—always eating over the pot and then wiping their mouths with the back of their hand. When they wanted more than just a taste, they tried to distract me by telling me a story or by saying that someone was looking for me at the front gate. I knew that they were lying so I never left the kitchen; instead I pretended not to see what they were doing—not for their sake but for my mother's. It was only later that I realized that it was then that the essence of my relationship with my mother began to form: even if it meant pretending, I had to make sure that she did not get hurt.

When some of the people who shared our home left and new neighbors moved in I worried that they were going to hurt us. I had heard about such goings on in other people's homes. Mariana's mother was beaten by Mr. Popescu who came home drunk one night and mistook her for his wife. At least that was what Mariana told me when I was over there one day while they were putting locks on their bedroom door.

Our new housemates were very different from the previous ones. They came with their own pots and pans, made their own meals, and never took anything from us. A young couple, the Moldovans, moved into my grandmother's sunroom. Mr. Moldovan worked for the railway station and Mrs. Moldovan was a saleslady. A Jewish couple from out of town moved into our dining room. Mr. Beck was a pharmacist, Mrs. Beck was a great storyteller. I tried getting a story out of her almost every day. "Have you been a good girl," she would ask, and even if I answered truthfully she would still tell me a story.

A highly placed party member and his wife moved into the upstairs guest-room. When he was not drunk, Mr. Munteanu liked to recite poems dedicated to the Communist Party. He recited these poems with great fervor and in a very loud voice so nobody could escape hearing him. Of course, nobody ever dared to complain. To do so one would risk being called a reactionary, an anarchist or even an enemy of the people. And that could get you into prison, no questions asked. When we did not hear Mr. Munteanu reciting his poems we could almost bet on hearing his wife scream at some point during the night because Mr. Munteanu was drinking and beating her. At times, we could hear Mrs. Munteanu run down the stairs to a neighbor who would take her in. Sometimes she slept in our room with my mother and me.

All these people shared the kitchen with us. There was only one big stove and one oven but everyone had their own table and part of what seemed to me then to be a huge cupboard. Until Mrs. Moldovan had her little girl, I was the only child around and I loved being in the kitchen while all the women were preparing meals and talking to each other about recent events or solving one another's problems. But the best time was in the evening when guests stopped by and a whole world came alive in that crowded room.

Two women came practically every night: Margareta, the judge's wife, who had great stories from the courtroom, and Hilde, who came with her dog Hexe (witch, in German) and talked about friends who had somehow managed to leave Romania and lived in Germany. My mother had stories about friends living in Israel or in America. Sometimes she read passages from letters she had received and then for a while everyone speculated about the writer. Was she happy? Was she telling the truth? What was her new life really like?

I was always sorry when I had to leave the kitchen to finish my homework or go to sleep. Though the kitchen was far from my bedroom and other noises interferred, I often left my door open in order to catch the end of a story or the beginning of a new one. My room was closer to the sunroom where Mr. Moldovan tried to listen "in secret" to Voice of America or Free Europe. The radio stations were so badly scrambled that one rarely heard anything but static. And yet, Mr. Molodovan never gave up.

One night, after leaving the kitchen—not because it was late but because I had to rise early the next morning for a school field trip—I woke up when I felt someone touching me. Mr. Munteanu was sitting on my bed. I had no idea how long he had been there but I was terrified, and when I tried to shout, he immediately stood up and told me that if I dared to tell anyone, my mother would go to prison just as my father had. He said that everyone knew that we did not like having him and his family in our house, and that people like us made up stories just to have more room for ourselves or to make room for Jews from out of town.

"Never!" I promised, "I'll never tell anyone."

And I didn't, until almost thirty years later. After the fall of communism and the death of Ceaușescu, I returned to that house in Romania, but my journey did not lead me home. Instead, I found release from the burden of silence.

# Mirka and I

(excerpt from an autobiographical novel, *The Edge of the Field*)

## Helen Degen Cohen/Halina Degenfisz

*The future: The Ghetto's population will shrink from 5,000 to 500, due to the Selections, where people are marched out of the Ghetto six abreast down the middle of a street, to the outskirts of town, where a man separates them, left and right, with those going to the right taken into the field and shot, and those to the left, returning to the Ghetto. The narrator's father, who works full time at survival, will find a way of getting his wife and child out of the Ghetto—the first of several feats that will get the family through the war. Mirka and her family will be shipped out of town, along with the remaining 500.*

NOTE: *Mirenka, not to be confused with Mirka, is the narrator's dead sister, to whom the entire book is told.*

"Mother?"
"Yes."
"What happened when the Germans came to Grojec?"
"When they came to Grojec, we escaped to Lida. I told you this."
"What happened when they came to Lida? When you used to embroider shirts?" Sitting on the bed, sewing shiny X's into penciled leaves and flowers and humming . . . waiting for him to come home. Those lonely evenings, lamplit and warm.

"What happened. They put us in a Ghetto, that's all."

They made one street into a Ghetto, put a dangerous fence around it, and all the Jews had to leave their apartments and were packed into the Ghetto, and the whole rest of the town was clean of Jews. It was a piece of street, that's all.

"Then what happened?"

"What do you mean what happened. We just lived in the Ghetto, that's all. We had a room with the Katzes, a doctor and his family, with a hanging sheet between us, and at night we went to bed on our side and they went to bed on their side."

"Didn't they have a daughter my age?"

"Yes, I told you."

*The Katzes had a daughter your age.*

And her name was Mira, but they called her Mirka, and we played . . . we had glass beads of all colors, and we made rings by weaving them together, and we even made bracelets. The beads were smaller than grain, small as seeds, a sand of crystals in a palm, and we wove them into rings, one bead wide, two beads wide, making the centers three and sometimes four beads wide, and they sparkled like rainwater, sparkled in our pockets, on our middle fingers, in our eyes—more beautiful than anything. Wait, was it with Stashia and Tereska? No, Mirka was Jewish, that is why we lived in the Ghetto, that is where we made the glass bead rings. But Mirka was different, Mirka was dark and sallow, with black eyes and straight black hair that stuck to her head in one oozy piece, and Mirka moved slowly, bending over like a string of black licorice, dreaming. She was never afraid. Because she loved her father. Mirka was very dark and very very Jewish. I was only Jewish. In a mirror, next to Mirka I was fat and fair, with thick fly-away brown hair, which Mama braided and I had to keep patting down, while Mirka's hair was oily and stuck to her. Mirka was thin, Mirka was all glued together and she moved and talked like glue, and she knew that her father loved her.

How did she know?

Mirka? Her father was rich, from being a doctor, she said. His skin was so thick and rich that it made me sick, but Mirka loved his skin, she would glue her cheek to his skin and rub on it... and he would kiss her with his thick lips and stare at her with his half-closed oily eyes. Mirka's eyes too were half closed, but "My parents are practical," she bragged. Her father gave Mirka a real gold ring, because her father had brought what he could carry with him into the Ghetto, secretly, and what he could carry with him was rich. He gave her a gold ring and promised her more, she said.

Mirka was lucky. Sometimes listening to her made me tired, but still she was lucky. My father had never given me a gold ring, my father had never even spanked me. Mirka's father spanked her, Mirka's father loved her. He spread his face slowly into a smile, like spilled oil, and Mirka melted into it. He was always there, and when he wasn't, she had his ring to prove that he loved her. While I floated in the gloomy air of the street, trying to attach myself to something, to Mirka, who escaped me into her father's smile. Who *was* my father? Mama said, "He is working every minute—you will see, he will do something." "Working?" "Every minute. Like a wild man. You will see. He will find a way." Her leg went back and forth, back and forth, like a machine. Who was my *mother*? They were so different from other people's parents, so—indescribable! Were all parents different from all other parents, or just mine! I had no more nails to bite off my fingers.

But Mirka and her parents and all of us were locked in by the same fence—"it wasn't like this before, like this street, was it, Mama? I can't remember"—and at night I was locked with my parents in the same bed, and Mirka with hers. In another Ghetto we slept seven on a bed, people had bad smells and slept in their clothes and another smell was there, which they called women's blood. That Ghetto didn't last too long, but I kept on smelling it. Women's blood.

We were in this place because we were Jewish. I had not understood it, this being Jewish. It hadn't meant living in the Red House and watching the gypsies at the door, or sitting in the park under the trees, or Mama's humming while she curled ladies' hair at the beauty shop—it was opposite to those things. It wasn't praying, like my grandfather prayed over his black-and-white stripes, was it? because Tata's father never prayed, nor my mother and father, and still they were Jewish, they were here. It wasn't eating cholent at Grandma's, because we never ate cholent at the Red House. It wasn't really being dark haired. Mama was red haired. But all the children who came to the fence from the fields were blonde, so maybe the blonder you were the less Jewish. Was Mama less Jewish? Was Mirka more Jewish? It meant being carried on wagons and trains, many times, and being taken by farmers across borders, and being locked up. And now that we were all together—*all together*—I looked around me at the word "Jewish." It meant being all together; and apart from others, in a Ghetto. It meant being dark with gold in your skin, being dark and dreamy and practical, because Mirka and her parents were very Jewish. What was "very Jewish"? And I looked closely at Mirka and was afraid of her, because she was so Jewish she didn't even think about it, as if she didn't know she was living in a Ghetto—so dreamy, so slow and smiley, and when I looked at her I thought, it's because she loves her father so much, and he loves her—being Jewish must mean loving your father so much that you forget you are Jewish.

"My father has a gold watch," she said, "you should see it . . . it is carved on both sides, and he said he would give it to me. . . ." I tried to imagine my father giving me a gold watch, his love for me melting in his eyes, but I couldn't.

"Let's go, let's do something," I'd say, but Mirka kept repeating, "He may give it to me for my birthday, and he has a silver locket. . . ." And so we would go nowhere, and I would sit there looking at Mirka, the air full of her sleepiness, and all I could see for hours afterward was Mirka's straight black hair hanging from her dark face tilted to one side, and so sad was the tilt, and so uncomfortable sometimes, that I had to keep straightening mine, that Jewish tilt, and running to ask Mama for something to eat—

*A doctor's daughter . . .*

She spilled beads into my hand, and I into hers, and we sat there choosing our transparent little colors, three blue, two yellow, two pink, and one green, weaving our rings in the street's only sunlight, that peculiar Ghetto sunlight, Mirka and I, neither of us sitting with the other, yet sitting so close to each other.

Go play with Mirka, *the doctor's daughter.* . . .

"Let's go for a walk," I said. "No," she said, "the street is dirty." Mama said the same thing. "But I want to see," I said, and finally she would follow me. From a distance we watched the bad boys: spitting in the street, turning toward a wall, chasing paper. Some sat on the curb playing their mysterious games, flipping stones or something. A girl walked by twisting her dress, then ran off. Some children were sailing paper boats in a puddle and we went to watch them. A girl was folding a yellowed sheet of newspaper into a new boat. We moved up closer.

At home I showed Mama how to do it but she wasn't paying attention, she gave up and walked away. So I ran out to show Mirka. But Mirka said she was tired and slinked away, her hands behind her back, the finger of one hooked into the finger of the other. So I sat there watching the others by myself, watching the rainwater drying in the dusty sun, or on some days, meandering past us in ripples and driblets, out of the Ghetto.

One day Mirka came out and we watched a group of children make a circle around the boy with the whooping cough—he bent over dripping foam and they looked at each other and made little noises and funny faces. The sun hurt our eyes. A mother came out looking for the boy and chased the others away. They should have been told it was contagious, to go away home, my mother said. Contagious. She meant that it could kill you, probably, but she never told me. She never told me what happened in the world. The children tried going back to their houses, but found this or that on the way because at home their parents would be sitting and waiting, waiting for something to happen, for the soldiers to come—a selection.

So they came out again and tripped and teased each other, and ran round and round each other, shouting. Phe on them all. They were all contagious, all of them. Except for Mirka.

And me of course. You could catch whatever they had, but you couldn't catch something like being fat, or Jewish. Tata had typhus once, and Mama saved him, without catching it. She knew how to do it. Catching it would make people stand in a circle and stare at you. Mama kept me away from it.

Go, go play with Mirka....

Beginning and finishing our glass-bead rings. When we ran out of beads, we took the rings apart and made new ones, or saved the beads for next time, some of them still threaded, in little papers in our pockets.

"Let's go to the fence," I said, "and look at the field." Mirka said no. I stood alone looking out at the field. Far off, to where they lived. If Mama found me here she would pull on me gently. "Ah, there is nothing to see, come back in the house." But she didn't pull me away too often, so it must not be so bad, standing here, it wasn't contagious. I stood at the fence touching the safe places between barbs, the diamond patterns the fence made, the thorns separating me from the field, and sometimes in the distance I saw them running, chasing, and sometimes running toward me, and I stood back, and I looked back around me, into the Ghetto.

Already a few Ghetto children were coming to see, coming to the fence, and I wanted to squeeze through them and run home, but also to remain standing there among them, facing the blonde ones with their mean faces, unwashed as the fields, wheat haired and raw skinned with bleached eyes, running and skipping toward us, their clothes ragged—how they ran to see us! Barefoot. And we were not, we still had shoes. They were bending down, looking for stones, something to throw, while still looking up at us... how they wanted to throw things at us, how good it must feel, maybe like throwing stones into water, to make it ripple and separate... and I stepped back, and turned around to see the dark ones behind me, and I squeezed through them and ran. Turned back around to look at them again, and ran. Turned, and ran.

And I never made it home, I had to stop and watch from a distance, wanting to still be there with the dark ones, among my own kind, to be the bravest one, the one in front of the others. The blonde ones were not so many, after all, only four or five, and suddenly they stood watching us, and the stones dropped from their hands, and instead of stones, they hurled words from their mouths, confusing words made of illness and blood and spoiled meat, as they watched us, even more fascinated than we were, spitting anger out of their mouths, dirty Jew and filthy Jew, and I touched, as if for the first time, the yellow patch on my sleeve. I too was a Jew.

And I wasn't alone, as I turned around, still imagining being the one in front, and turning around, they were throwing the words at all of us together, I must look like one of the dark ones behind me, the ones my mother had said were contagious. But I am not like the others, I am only fat, and I am very important really, I can dance and sing, I know so many things. They were no different from me. Mama could be wrong, I could be just like the sick ones in the street, like the ones who sailed boats in the puddle, and like Mirka—who loved her father. Even if I had no gold ring. Loved her father. The sick one. The dark one. We were all the same. I had thought no one was like me, which was good and bad and untrue. But was it? I belonged to the dark ones—dance or sing or read poems out of books, nothing would have helped. Nothing? I had never known this.

"Dirty, pissy, scummy Jews," said the tall blonde girl scratching her head, yellow coming from her nose, the bigger boy in a torn shirt and mud-stained baggy pants, the other boy with his hand between his legs, the small girl rubbing her eye with a dirty hand. "Scum," they said, quietly now. "Dirty Jew." Some of the words I didn't know. They must be Christian words, not Polish. I looked at the smaller girl, my size, wanting her to see me, I was not dirty, wanting to whisper "Look at me." She spat in my direction. And I turned and squeezed through the "scum" behind me, who were just beginning to talk back which scared me even more, because the fields had made them stronger, and the street had made us weaker, and their voices could be heard across the fields, while sometimes we had to whisper. I squeezed through the weak scum for the second time that day, or third... when finally nothing was clear, or true, not even the Red House I had lived in—

"Irenka?" Mama said, from where she was cooking. I looked away. "Irenka," she said, "we will have a birthday party tomorrow, in the afternoon maybe."

*Photos light up in the dark, not faces but photographs, ghosts of photographs, no color, only sepias and grays. We could lock ourselves up with the odor of film, Mirenka, chewing our nails, removing layers of days and nights.*

*And trains. One of those trains passed by here, taking all our photographs. All. Strange, that a few of us are here, but none of the photos. "All the pictures are gone." Mama sets the fact on the table. I believe her. There are so few pictures in her eyes, thick panes of glass over them. "Pictures?" "Death is an undeveloped negative," said Uncle—who? Mirenka, ... is it really very still and totally empty... doesn't some of the color come up, out of water, and the still shapes? Oh, Mirenka, does it really have no walls or floors or ceilings or—boundaries? No beginning or end? To have no walls ever? No Red House ever, no walls? Nothing to hold onto, nothing to touch? Not the smallest anchor, in all of space? Not even a negative?*

*All I need, to live, is my Red House. The table, the chair, the food, the mother and father, the window with the tree in it. When I bleed, the house bleeds down to the ground—is... What is death, Mirenka*

Here is my birthday party in the Ghetto, taken from the inside out. Mama has found marmalade somewhere, she is spreading it on, and the tea is steaming in tall glasses. Mirka is there, and another child whose face is lost. The Katzes are looking in, from around the corner of the sheet. They have never seen a party in the Ghetto. In the window are faces, steaming up the glass with their breath, the whites of their eyes enlarged. I don't know what to do with them, so I'm taking pictures, something in me is taking pictures, pictures I will never develop, of faces I'll never remember. Are they jealous? As long as I can remember, Mama has given me a birthday party, but never like this one, this one with its undeveloped faces. "Look, Mama." She hesitates, ach, she waves her hand. Mrs. Katz comes to me, slimy warm, and says, "Irenka," putting her hands on me, "have many, many more happy birthdays." She is sloppy—I want to say No, go away, Mrs. Katz, this is my birthday! I look around at the people enjoying my birthday. I'm the fat one to whose party they came, I'm the fat one in the picture, I am not like those at the puddle, I'm the fat one and I'm no one, I am one of those faces. "I don't want any more bread and jam." "But why, Irenka?" "I don't want to." "Don't be silly, Irenka, finish your bread come, come." Mama is smiling, embarrassed, everyone is smiling. I look hard at the lights in the glass of marmalade, till the room is sweet in them, till the warmest light shines through the glass of tea, and Tata comes in, with honey.

I stand at the edge of the field, looking through diamonds of space—the wind really lets you smell the field, the smells of sunset, then of night coming. Behind me some children are sick, probably from getting too close to each other. They are hungry, the blonde ones who will soon be here. Why do they come here if they don't like us? There is something so strange about it. Whoever stands here at this moment, whoever is Jewish at this moment, stands facing those children and their stones. And only here does it happen, not when you stand facing the town, or your parents, or the food on the table, or the month of May in America. Only here. As if here were my only home. But no one is with me, and already it is getting dark. I am the only one here. Move, idiot, the dark whispers, coming in quickly now, go play where you belong, go play with Mirka, Mirka will not hurt you.

Mirka?

Mirka has a gold watch now, whose hands keep pointing to wherever they want on the earth, as it ticks ts-ts-ts-ts-ts-ts-ts-ts-ts-ts-ts-ts-ts.

# Independence Park: A Fiction

## Dina Elenbogen

### 1991 Jerusalem

The Arab in Independence Park says I am a mistrustful woman. He knows this by the way I clench my fist, wrap my arms around my stomach, and look everywhere but into his eyes. I did not invite him to share this park bench with me nor did I tell him that last week I buried my mother near the Mt. of Olives. I do not tell him it is the noise on the border or the way I fall too quickly in love when I turn Jerusalem corners, that has made me the way that I am. Instead I tell him he is wrong, must be wrong until he proves that I can't trust. He asks me to leave my bag on the grass, to let go of everything I have, to let him take my hand and push it until it opens into a beautiful, trembling, flower.

I tell him I have played this game before and lost. I have opened like a flower only to be pulled from the soil the way he has been removed from his land. I tell him I have trusted strangers and that is why I live with my arms wrapped around my belly, why I push away everything, even love, before it has had a chance to blossom.

### 2001 Chicago

The Arab at Mercy Hospital who stands at the end of my bed where I am pushing out my son says I am a strong woman. My arms are wrapped around my husband's body to shield me from the pain, to bring him into it. It is not a conscious decision to trust this Palestinian American doctor named Jacob at the foot of my bed but I do. I let go of everything, all control of my bowels, my manners. I let go of my husband and this man rests his fist on my pleasure spot; for a moment he takes my pain. It is only later that I wonder if I can take his pain with my hands but I know it does not live in his body.

Outside it is storming and my son's insistence on entering the world this night, one month early, pulls Jacob out of another woman's room where he is gloved and masked, prepared to cut her baby from her womb. He is called to my bedside where only my son and I know that he is about to enter the beginning of the world. I push and push and over the nurse's shrieks Jacob's voice is clear and low, a soothing melody. He tells me I am a strong woman and I can do this. I believe him and push my son into Jacob who catches him and offers my husband a tool with which to cut the umbilical cord. As if this is the end of the story Jacob tells me he must leave now, and return to the woman in the next room.

The woman in the next room, Rachel, still thinks Jacob is a Jew. Her midwife says he is the only doctor she knows who treats midwives with respect. The other doctors push them aside to attend to difficult births. So because of his manner and his name, Rachel never considered that he wasn't a Jew. I have just learned this news myself when Jacob's name appeared on the list of who would step in for my midwife if I should deliver while she was away. My husband knew right away that he was Arab.

    This was not a problem for me. But for Rachel, who I met in my prenatal Yoga class, I knew it would be different. Over the past few months as we watched our bellies expand in the dim candle light created by our yoga instructor, Rachel, another American Jew, told me the story of why she had returned from her settlement in the West Bank, not far from Ramallah, where it turns out Jacob was born. When she was pregnant with her first child, a Palestinian burst into her home one night on a random rampage. He tried to stab Rachel and her husband jumped in front to protect her. He was killed along with their unborn child. But her dreams of what Israel could be were not buried with her family. She remained and married again. When she became pregnant with their first child she returned to Chicago so her mother could be with her while she gave birth. Although I am against the occupation of the territories and Rachel has built a home in them, we bonded the way potential and new mothers bond while we learned stretches that were supposed to make labor and delivery easier for us. We never imagined that my water would break on the same day that she was brought in for a Cesarean. I will not tell Rachel that the man who is returning to her room with a mask, the man who will protect her unborn child who is two weeks late by performing a C-section, is not a Jew but an Arab.

My son sleeps a lot but I am not well. My vision is blurry and my body is in shock from the quickness with which life passed through it. My mother is not here to tell me it will be okay or to remind me of her story—how quickly I came into the world. She had left Palestine for America because she thought it would be easier to be a wife here and a mother and because she thought that maybe she had fallen in love with an American man who was visiting the kibbutz where she lived in the center of the country. This man became my father.

But when my mother was here she didn't say that much. English was not her mother tongue and my Hebrew is biblical. So I would imagine what she might say. What she would think. Maybe I put my own thoughts into her head. Maybe I only imagined that she was always longing for the land of her youth, a past love or maybe even a lost idea. As I hold my son to my breast I want to know my mother's own thoughts, not my father's translations, not my projections. Now that I am a mother I want my own mother back, but she is gone. I do not know yet that I have been captured by the Arab's sad eyes, that they will calm me and cause restlessness, that I will pack a bag.

Jacob comes to see me again and again. When he walks in my hospital room I pull my gown in false modesty to cover my breasts, my belly. He tells me not to, that he wants to feel my stomach to see if my body is returning back to its prepregnant state. His hands are so gentle I forget they are there until I feel the pleasure, the first thing I have felt besides loss since my son's birth. On each visit we go over my birth story as if to serve as witnesses for each other, that it really happened as we think it did: my son came out in a flash of lightning, and in that same flash we recognized something in one another that allowed us to speak in hushed tones and to hear each other amid my screams, to look into each other and feel the ache of the past. And during each visit we understood more deeply that we are not like doctor and patient, or father and daughter like Jacob and Dinah in the Bible. We share a motherland where my mother rests and Jacob's mother waits for him, where the future is unreadable.

My room empties of my husband who must return to his duties. I am now in postpartum and Rachel is down the hall healing from her surgery. Her mother has not left her side. When I see the joy in their eyes as they pass Rachel's son back and forth, I know that for them it no longer matters where Jacob was born. Their love has already grown deeper than their pain.

I wonder what my mother would think about my son's dark skin and deep blue eyes. I wonder, too, about her birth story, how she stopped in the middle of labor to put on hose although it was August and after midnight, how quickly I came into the world, how quickly my mother left it. I stare into my mother's silence and Jacob returns to replay my birth story and in the silence that comes in between our words he tells me the story of his birth, in the country where my mother was born and buried, the country he calls Palestine, the country I call Israel.

Jacob says that if he were a woman he would want to give birth the way that I did—where you don't know what hit you—where the baby's movement through your body is torrid yet short-lived. And when he says this, I wonder if like me he lives half his life in his imagination and if in his other life he is a woman. And I wonder if maybe that's why women fall in love with Jacob, because he can imagine the life of a woman.

It is the eighth day, the Brit Mila of my son, the covenant of the flesh. Our living room is filled with uncles, brothers, and fathers—our mothers are dead. The other women are whispering far enough away from the knife that will remove the foreskin from my son's penis. I am thinking of Jacob and of Isaac being sacrificed at the altar, of the intervening angel. We have given our son the name Isaac. I never thought to ask why we still partake in this barbaric ritual until this moment, but it is too late. The rabbi cuts my son's foreskin and my question resonates in the angry eyes of my husband whose head is covered with an embroidered skull cap. Even after my son stops crying I cannot stop my own tears. The rabbi asks me to leave the room with my son and to suckle the pain from his body. And I do leave the room and pack a bag with one cotton dress and nothing else but diapers for my son. He will live off my breast. Yes, I do leave the room as the rabbi has asked: I leave the room, our house, a country.

 I sit in the blue room where all of my books are and dream of Jacob. I believe that he can protect me, that because he knows the suffering of women he can protect us from ourselves. After our son was born I realized that my husband and I could not protect our marriage. My father was unable to save my mother from her illness and so my mother was not here to shield me from the pain of childbirth and the pain that comes after. She was not leaning over my bed telling me her secret or the secret of survival. It is only in my dreams that she comes to me, just back from a faraway journey, a packed bag in her hands.

No, my mother was not there to help me push my son into this world, to assure me I could do it. My husband was there and I held onto him for dear life and he told me I could do it, but he didn't promise that afterward I would be the same. And when I wasn't the same he no longer knew how to speak to me.

Jacob had stepped in just when I thought I could no longer bear the pain. He listened to my screams and he listened to my whispers as if they were the first sounds ever of a woman trying to bring life into the world. He stood there strong and certain that I would pull through and he would still know me afterward. He told me I was a strong and trusting woman.

While the men downstairs drink Schnapps, I sit in my blue room with a packed bag drinking liters of mineral water like Jacob said to. I do whatever he says because he did not let me die in childbirth. When Isaac came out though everything changed. My heart burst open yet I could not love my husband or soothe my crying child. I thought of Jacob and how sweet, oh so sweet exile can be. When he touches me I lose everything that I think I should have become: a wife, a mother—and I am a woman again. Oh, how sweet, this exile.

*The country we are leaving for eight days after Isaac's birth is the country where Jacob was born and where my mother was born and rests. In the twilight after birth we had joked about how we are from the same country, how in the Old Testament Jacob is Dinah's father, not her lover. And we agreed on this: We are not free in America. Jacob's real name is Hassan but he has only saved the letter "H," which he places in front of his name.*

*I have removed the letter "H" from the end of my name so that I am the American "Dina" and no longer Jacob's daughter in the Bible. Hassan goes by the name H. Jacob so Jewish women will come to him and have their babies. And women do come to him and after he delivers their babies and they fall in love with his sad eyes they return to their husbands. With me, Jacob says, he knew it would be different. I would pack a bag and take my son who he delivered because it is the thread that has connected us. He knew he would need to show me the land of his boyhood where over a decade ago I walked through Independence Park, where an Arab accused me of being a weak and mistrustful woman.*

*We do not have a name for this country. I call it Israel and Jacob, who goes by Hassan, calls it Palestine. We settle on Jerusalem as we stroll through Independence Park not holding hands. We will go to Ramallah to visit his mother who wants to die in Palestine, who with her eyes tells him not to trust me. I am not just an American; I am a Jew. We will visit my mother's grave where her body was sent, on her request, after she died in America. As a young woman she left Israel by choice. Hassan Jacob left, he says, because he had no choice. My people were devouring his land and his dreams.*

*My mother had her babies in America. We grew up so fast dreaming of Israel that I forgot to ask her why we give birth so fast and why it is so hard to be a wife and a mother.*

*I forgot to ask her why we are always leaving a room.*

Even after I stopped living in my head with Jacob I couldn't tell you how he feels about Jews, about Arabs and Jews. In all of the conversations we did and did not have, in all of the conversations I imagined, we never discussed the politics of land or of peace. We discussed our mothers more than our motherlands. We returned there together in my fantasy, where I lost Jacob to his sadness and his mother's mistrust. We never spoke of what belongs to whom and we never passed blame. Instead we tried to remove the pain from one another although we learned our pain can be deeper than our love.

*Even in my dream Hassan will go back to America to become Jacob who delivers Jewish babies. I will stay awhile to wait for my mother's answers. It is not until I am in the air between the two countries that I hear my mother's voice. It is not until I am on my way back to my husband, a room, a country that the rhythm of her words flow from the song I sing my son as I soothe him back to sleep.*

Jacob, who delivered my son, delivered me from the pain that comes after childbirth, the pain we don't speak of as loudly as we do the pain of pushing out life.

# Burning in Cuba

## JYL LYNN FELMAN

*Incantation I*

*I am born between the legs of three screaming women sweating.*

*In 1954 I am born in three places at once. Three wombs stretch open howling with pain birthing me into (a) howling pain.*

*I am born between the heavy hot legs of three screaming women sweating.*

*I am born in the rhythms of a river of blood.*

*From Spain to Cuba*

*I am born in blood but do not speak the language.*

*Crossing the Atlantic*

*To the center of the Caribbean Sea. I do not speak.*

*I bleed.*

*From the wombs of three women I bleed women. Knowing that the revolution will never make me free. Because. Solidarity always stops at the border and bleeding women are never free.*

When I am 50 years old I go to Cuba for the first time. A special visa is required to cross the border. Only an official license will let me in.

At *Museo de Bellas Artes* I start in the *Contemporary Art* section. A woman painted dark brown seated on a hard wooden chair holding her infant daughter is the first painting I stand in front of. I read the name of the painting, *Maternidad 1954*. And stare at what I see. The hard wooden chair sits firm on the tightly packed dirt floor while I sleep protected in my mother's arms.

In the *Colonial Period* the last painting I see (before leaving the museum) is a woman painted white sitting in a comfortable green-cushioned chair holding her infant daughter. I read the name of the painting, *Maternidad 1954*. And stare at what I see. The green chair rocks gently back and forth while I sleep in my mother's arms, safe.

*In Cuba I am born in three places at once. From the colored wombs of three screaming women I am born in quietude with a scream inside my mouth.*

I am born in 1954. On the Jewish Sabbath. In the midst of war fleeing families cross borders. They cross because of us. You and I. In the midst of war babies are born. On the other side. I am born in a Catholic hospital called "Good Samaritan" with Jesus nailed tightly to the cross that hangs on the pale pink wall above my fleeing mother's Jewish head.

Fleeing families don't know how to stop.

*In Cuba I am born painted brown sweating and dripping blood between the hot heavy legs of three screaming women. Queen Isabella shakes her royal blue head while glaring down at me.*

*In Spain I am born the color of impure sand. Jewish families hide. Pretending to cross the border. We convert. Fleeing families never stop. While the light of Shabbas candles slips out of locked doors from inside dark closets in damp basements that smell of mold. The light always slips through. The light slips through.*

*In Dayton I am born a Jew and have no color but the closet is no longer locked. Only fleeing families don't know how to stop. When closets are unlocked the border closes in. Jews in shame hide in locked closets with the light showing through. Borders close.*

*The Jew hides.*

I do not speak a word.

*All my life (I feel) Jesus bows his head and points his chin at me. I want to understand the strange man who lives his life nailed forever to a cross on pale pink Catholic walls. Does it hurt? Drying blood leaves a stain. He says. From sea to shining sea.*

*He says.*

*No one ever forgets. How much it hurts. The stain of drying blood. And the memory of the pain.*

*I never forget.*

*The memory of the pain of drying blood staining my body red. The people don't forget. But does it have to hurt forever? Hurt forever? From sea to shining sea drying blood always leaves a stain. He says.*

In Cuba I buy a painting, a print by a man named "Jesus" that is of a woman and two heads—"Doble Personalidad." It is beginning to

Burning in Cuba ❖ 45

make sense. A U.S. passport. A Cuban visa. A Jewish passport always searching for a visa.

*I am born at the border between the choking smell of human flesh burning and the sounds of angry young boys slinging rocks. I am born between wailing walls made of stone and turquoise temple mounts. I am born between tiny grains of impure sand. I am born Jewish in a Catholic hospital with Jesus watching over me. I am born hot between the colored legs of every woman's hidden lust for her sister and the border of the big almighty phallus blocking the way. I am born "Doble Personalidad" on the border line on every border that exists.*

*I am born between tiny grains of sand on the border of double personalities. Each time I am born I am born "Doble Personalidad."*

*The border is sand.*

*Dunes of sand disappear. Into other dunes that rise up again. Rising and falling. Falling and rising. Winds blow. From all directions. Sand flies. Walls rise. Dunes of sand disappear.*

*The wind blows.*

*And the passion of Jesus drips his blood on me. Crossing the border that is my Jewish female body. Crossing the body that is the border between you and me.*

*Sand catches in my eyes.*

*Walls rise again. The wind blows. I can no longer see. Solidarity stops at the border of bones living and dead. I can not cross shattered bones. The bones of shattered people never rise again.*

*But the bones chatter.*

*Bones chatter. Knocking against each other the bones chatter. Knocking bones chatter. Listen. Listen to the bones left at the border. Knocking. Chattering into the cold night air. Listen. They shiver at the border waiting. Bones chatter knocking. Knocking bones chatter.*

*Listen.*

In Cuba there is a painting, oil on canvas of a brown woman with burnt red lips and coal black eyes full of yellow sockets. She doesn't speak to those who stare. On her head she carries large overripe mangoes split right down the middle (and) painted red on the inside.

Big black seeds push up

from hard centers of overripe mangos. Falling out her ears the mangoes balance on (her) shoulders resting peacefully midair. Mangoes fall one after another out of white headdresses wrapping the round heads of the women who carry small piles of overripe mangoes cut open and painted red on the inside.

Black seeds push up.

Inside the mangoes are painted red (not yellow). They are bleeding. Have you ever seen a mango bleed out of the head of a woman made of sand?

*Incantation II*

*Tongue to Tongue*

*The first boundary is the tongue. The tongue-like lips hanging at the vortex between my legs between my mother's tongue waiting to be licked and sucked hard. The first boundary is the tongue. The tongue right inside my mouth. Is waiting. The tongue waits to cross the border(s). From Africa to Cuba.*

Burning in Cuba ❖ 47

*In and out. From Spain to Cuba. Over and under. From Hamburg to Habana. From Gaza to Elat. Back and forth in and out over and under. From the West Bank and Bethlehem. Sucking and licking the wet tongue sucks its way across forbidden borders.*

*To Jerusalem.*

*While always and at the same time knowing she is crossed by other tongues. Forbidden and not forbidden. The tongue sits behind white teeth waiting. The lips like tongues guard the entryway between a woman's legs and her many colored mouths.*

*The boundary is the first tongue. The tongue-like lips hanging at the vortex between my legs between my mother's tongue waiting to be licked and sucked hard. The first boundary is the tongue. The tongue right inside my mouth. Is waiting. The tongue waits to cross the border(s). Mouth to mouth. Hers to Hers. In and out. From Breast to buttocks.*

*Over and under.*

*Open hand to tight fist. Back and forth in and out over and under faster and faster. Open hand to hard fist fucking blood. Sucking and licking the wet tongue sucks its way across forbidden borders. From inside a woman's deep desire for her sister. While always and at the same time knowing she is crossed by other tongues. Forbidden and not forbidden. The tongue sits behind white teeth waiting. The lips like tongues guard the entryway between a colored woman's legs and her many mouths.*

*Lips like tongues guard entryways.*

*My Jewish female the color of sand Spanish non converso tongue travels to Cuba all the way through dense borders thickened dark by thunderclouds ready to burst at the first sign of lightning streaking across the border of an azure sky.*

*Only my Jewish female tongue.*

*No habla español. No! No habla español my Jewish tongue. In Cuba I am. A woman. In Jerusalem I am not. A man.*

*Ani Adonoi Elocheha.*

*I am the Lord thy God who brought you out of the land of Egypt out of the house of bondage. I take my Jewish female non converso marano pig's tongue with me to Cuba. The Queen said I had to get out. Leave her precious country now or change the color of my Hebrew tongue.*

*There is a time when all I speak is Hebrew is all I speak. At 17 I am Che Guevara standing in the hot Jerusalem sun while my olive skin burns red. All my hair is pulled back. I have the picture. I can show you. My muscles as they start to grow. The muscles growing out of my arms prepare for revolutions that I do not understand. Living high in the Judean Hills I am Che. We. Che and I climb together. Up and down steep valleys freeing (all the) slaves while bleeding mangoes split open. Have you ever seen a bleeding mango split right down the center.*

In the picture that my first woman lover takes of me I am 17 years old standing on a mountain in the Judean Hills looking out at the land I love. The sky behind me is very blue and my Jewish skin turns olive brown beneath a red Jerusalem sun. I stand. Tall and erect dressed in navy blue shorts and a navy tank top. I wear a belt around my hips with a huge silver buckle. I gaze down ancient mountains to small villages to the middle of urban streets. Looking up I see the single dirt path leading to *Har Sinai*, the sacred mountaintop.

The woman warrior stands tall.

I am a *sabra*. A cactus tough and strong.

## Don't Touch Me.

Don't touch. The prick of needles go deep. A *sabra*. A native-born Israeli cut open. Sweet like mangoes juicy on the inside, succulent and bittersweet each bite.

On the back of the photo someone writes "The Female Che Guevara." At 17 I do not know who Che Guevara is only that he is important. Later, I find out that Che Guevara is the revolution. I have no idea what this means. At 17 I smile out at the people with the tart taste of satisfaction on my lips. Women warriors stand tall.

I know I am the revolution.

I have no idea what this means. At 17 I do not know who Che Guevara is. But I carry his picture with me always until I understand. I do not understand until I understand that all mangoes are red inside even if they taste yellow.

*In Cuba I walk the streets staring at the people, craving Hebrew tongues.*

*In the synagogue when I meet the Jews of Cuba there are no Jewish Cubans to meet. There are only Cuban Jews. As soon as we meet I long for the wetness of their Hebrew/Caribbean/Catholic Santeria tongues to moisten my own lost wandering tongue.*

*But the Cuban Jewish Jewish Cuban tongues of Jews of Cuba are unfamiliar to my eager taste. They pray in Hebrew sounding Spanish as they speak in tongues unrecognized. Praying from the siddur I read Spanish transliterated into Hebrew for the first time.*

*When I am 50.*

*I read Hebrew in Spanish in the shul in Habana on Erev Shabbat. This is how I learn to speak again. The woman who carries small piles of large mangoes on her head doesn't speak to those who stare. In Hebrew I speak Spanish for the first time. When I speak Hebrew in Spanish mangoes split open and turn red.*

*I am born between the legs of three screaming women who make no sound.*

*Screaming women giving birth do not make a sound.*

*There are no Jewish women writers left in Cuba.*

*Born between the legs of women I howl my entire life.*

*I am born*

*between the legs of three screaming women who do not make a sound. I am born howling with all the Jewish women writers. Jewish women howl at the borders of mangoes split open.*

It is as a *feminista Vilde Chaye wild beast* radical lesbian feminist Jew(ess) that I go to Cuba looking for the women of fleeing families who never stop. Handsome Sephardic sisters thrown out of Spain. Che is the revolution. Fidel said stay. Join with us. Or leave. And so *conversos* we become again. First time in Babylon. The second time is Spain. We learn Spanish. "Give me your tired, your poor hungry masses starving to be free." Jews hide with shame in dark closets. The St. Louis is always turned away. Light slips through dark closets

In Cuba I am.

In Cuba mangoes reside within the white headdresses of brown women.

I want inside the mango.

In Cuba. In Cuba I find (I am reborn). In Cuba In Cuba In Cuba. An incantation and a verb. In Cuba I. In Cuba I am I. . . . Cuba is a verb. Women loving other women's tongues have their tongues split open. Our tongues fall out. We do not rest in midair.

In Cuba I split open.

In Cuba the Hebrew tongues of my people slide with ease in and out of the synagogue. Every *Shabbas*. In Cuba the female tongues of the women I love do not slide with ease. They do not slide out when the mango splits open. They drop falling from midair straight to the ground and disappear. In Cuba I am and am not. I am not in Cuba, in Cuba I am a yellow mango painted red. Split open black seeds push up hard. And do not stop until they come. All the way. Through the other side black seeds push.

Women's tongues split open.

Finally. This is my voice. I can no longer write in full sentences. I never really could. But in fragments I can write. The imagination is not an ordered place. There are only red Jews in yellow synagogues speaking Hebrew in Spanish holding black seeds. Order in the imagination is impossible. In the imagination sentences do not survive.

Followed by small black dots.

That mark the beginning and the end. Between each sentence a single black dot marks the border. In the imagination the dots are never black. Nouns do not follow verbs. Or they will not survive.

Nouns are verbs. Cuba is a verb. Moving vertiginously . . . crossing the page Cuban Jews are proper nouns, never modifying adjectives or adverbs. Cuban Jews are red speaking Spanish in an ancient yellow tongue. Split open.

And the revolution in Cuba is still. In Cuba there is still revolution. Nouns become verbs the past tense is no more. There is only present tense. Even the conditional is gone. The revolution threw away all the rules of grammar. Today the pronouns they/he/she/it/you/them/us are subjects. Every sentence. I and Thou. I know I am not Cuban. I do not speak Spanish. I am afraid. What will happen (to me) if I speak Spanish. When I speak Spanish sand dunes disappear. In the wind the border moves again and reappears.

Black seeds mark the spot where yellow mangoes bleed.

*Im Eshkahach Yerushalyim, t'shcach y'meni.* If I forsake thee O Jerusalem may my right hand lose its cunning.

But I am the forsaken one. And all the woman's tongues are split. Right down the middle.

And yes Fidel is forever and yes Fidel has to go. Fidel forever Fidel must go. In Cuba there is one of everything. In Cuba there is only one Fidel. In Cuba I am and I am not. Fidel thinks he is a descendent of the Jews expelled from Spain. I read the letters from the front that Che wrote Commandante Camilo.

*Incantation III*

They write as they fight.

These men. Muscles fierce with revolution. They wrote as they fought. To each other. Letters. Of longing. Letters. Of longing. Back and forth. Che to Camilo. Camilo to Che. Che to Fidel. Fidel to Camilo. They wrote. Of a man's deep love. For another man. They wrote the battle. To take back Habana.

In Trinidad I read the letters. Stunned. I read what no one ever says. (In all this time.) It is so obvious. There are photos. Everywhere. On the walls. Sealed in cases. Smiling comrades wrap their arms around each other. Writing letters. Of Longing. As they fight.

Their eyes gleam out.

Preserved forever.

Under locked glass homoerotic revolutionary passion passes back and forth between good soldiers in difficult combat. I stare at the black-and-white photos.

Passion passes back and forth.

In the museum they preserve the letters. In the museum in Trinidad for Camilo. The letters of the revolutionaries and their visions are displayed. But they don't tell. The story. The other part. About the comrades who are *compañeros* who are in love and cross the fatal border. With each other. Because. There is (always) only one revolution at a time. That the people will tolerate and that good soldiers are willing to fight for.

One revolution is plenty.

But I saw the letters—saved and preserved Camilo to Che. Che to Fidel the brothers write back and forth sliding their pens like tongues across the matted page to each other. The brothers are writing still. When full moons rise Cuban Jews speak Hebrew in Spanish. But who does an aching Fidel turn his weary body to?

When full moons rise

Fidel turns his heavy lonely body in the middle of the night. But there is no one left. To kiss good night. And kiss. No one left. To kiss. Good night. And good night. And kiss. And kiss. Tongue to tongue. And back again. Good night.

There is no one left.

Fidel turns his heavy body to the wall and dreams of revolution. Kiss. Good night. And kiss. Moist tongues wet together never die. A comrade's tongue inside his brother is like no other. Cuba is a verb like no other without a future tense.

Fidel is the border from past to present.

There is no future after revolution. Fidel must never die. Fidel can not die. He doesn't know. How to die. But he knows. Under cover in the night the feel of his brother reaching. Camilo to Che. Meet crossing fields of battle. Fidel to Che. Warm bodies reach. In battle the brothers warm reaching hot. Hot brothers reach while crossing battled fields.

Fidel must never die.

Or the mangoes will never open yellow. Flying out the ears of Jewish women made of sand. Their wet tongues always forced to meet under cover in the night.

Still

Under cover in the night the moist tongues of women split mangoes and prepare to eat.

There are no more incantations.

# Homeland Security

## S. E. Gilman

### The Horse I Rode in On

Cleaning out my family home, we find photographs, most of them unmarked, of the dead and no one to tell us the names of the doughboys crouched next to our grandmother and her friends, she in long, dark, banana curls, the thin silk kerchief given until the boys came home, the unnamed boys. My mother might know but she passed away two, three years ago now. I do remember the black-and-white shots she took of us, me on the high chair and my big sister standing next to me, both holding turkey legs at Thanksgiving and my face greasy and happy gnawing on the bones. We pack boxes, sort the garage sale, we're told that the dealers find little of value—mismatched silver plate, the jelly glasses, broken victrola. We donate to the indigent new rags.

First our home is on the market, our home is sold. The key is given up, we drive away in separate directions, and there is no home to go home to anymore. Dig your way to China if you want to, but come back and there's no one to take you in. Childhood comes to rest in a photograph, in a cigar-box memento. Mama dies, Papa is sent to the old men's home. Home the Repository? I get that. But we comfort ourselves with our second childhood, back to the hearth goddess and the mythical patriarch. Mama dies, Papa in the Old Men's Home. Parental comfort, babyself fantasy, the desire, cooing, sinking back into unconsciousness, the dream of unconditional fog, oblivion or love.

The real story, my bubbies? Listen. We came by wagon and on swollen clubfoot from schtetl to schtetl, from ghetto to steerage, and before that, more wandering. Maybe the Spanish would make room, now maybe the Dutch. My people with their marks of separation, marks of the pride of distinction, of ukase, of litigation that said Jews cannot practice in the guilds or grow crops to sell or engage in medicine and touch a gentile. Never a home we couldn't lose, be expelled from, forced to kneel or go. Usually we went.

## Our New Land

To America, new homeland, a territory shared by or divided by a common language and two parties, the others encouraged to silence, to the packing of their bags—Emma Goldman in America but not for long, the union women in prison because business is business. A land of freedom where my father said in Miami Beach hotels signs in the Depression said "No Dogs and No Jews." But that was so long ago, wasn't it? Now it's a Red and Blue state of false dichotomy, forced choice, loaded questions: Do you want the terrorists to win? Fifty years ago Communists, a hundred years ago Socialists, Anarchists. Flags stuck on bumpers, windows, storefronts, as if that bit of adhesive explained Assimilation or Death. One real party is going on—Be White or be blue. All that red shed? No tears for weaklings that stood in Pullman's way or John D's steel then or Citibank's now. If the CEO, if the Board of Directors resides in the United Emirates or Antigua, by gum, sticky that little flag on your lapel, on your bowling ball, or you're a dirty coward dog to object so much as a yellow peep, you outside agitator, you class warrior. We do not teach real history. History is unpleasant, unseemly. Let me get you a drink.

## Lilith, Eve, Sarah, and Sylvia and Bella too

Land where my fathers died, where mothers sewed in sweatshops, or stayed put, put out sex for three squares and a proper male surname, watched her back when she went out if she belonged to no one. Grateful she was to have a home if he didn't hit her, didn't drink, or didn't run around. Isn't that enough for a woman? Does she keep her man as he keeps her? Trade for a little protection and a cut of the proceeds. Threats from without and within. Perverts, sourpusses, three-dollar queers? Keep your mouths shut. We're Normal, Red-Blooded, One Hundred Percent. Is mother secure? Half of apple-pie American mothers have no husbands, abandoned or had to leave, not widowed. Mothers and children are drains on manhood. What does mother do with her fatherless sons? Will they go loyally to the recruitment office when the factory shuts down or their uncle is not In Some Business? Sons can learn to be prison guards if we run out of wars. Are her daughters meek and chaste? Better hope so. Five in twenty daughters will be raped. What Homeland security? A deception, mother's milk and mock apple pie, made from Ritz.

## Orchards in the Promised Land

I brought my dimes to temple every week. I want to see my tree. Fifty years in Israel, the oldest of Old Countries, the original homeland, and there is no more talk of trees but walls, sectioning those separated from Jewish identity, Othering, perpetuating the grab for territory. Transparent when Americans called it Manifest Destiny, conquering the frontier, civilizing the savage, pushing inhabitants of that land to cordon themselves off to the most unforgiving margin. An accident of birth—are you chosen or savage? Statecraft made by suicide bombs, children's diplomacy with rocks and rifles, terror on the schoolbus just another day. Identity, not history, is bunk, Mr.

Ford. Martyrs made daily on the assembly line. With that kind of productivity, shouldn't we be rational by now? Israel some kind of example? We are—of victims who become abusers. It doesn't take a prophet to see this shit. Put the bottle down or die of thirst, put the rifle down or die of self-righteousness. My tree is a burned-out spar, a bludgeon, a bitter fruit.

## Real and Bunk

Homeland? Deceit. Illusion. A pretense to cover our wanderings, our temporality. In truth there is no place to come home to but our drifting, changing homelands that are only dry rocks on which to rest, imaginary homelands across continents and centuries. Jews long separated by law and custom carried a portable culture, outsiders. So my bags are already packed, I was born packed, and my babushka is at the door. You can't hit a moving target, they say. But women, women with children must stay home. I will defend if I must stay. Women make homes to protect children from those Horsemen as if the breast were home enough, the body the shelter. She will be drained, be broken, pass away.

In truth we are homeless and should know it deep. We are refugees always. Mama dies, Papa Yahweh's in the Old Man's Home. Homelessness is our true condition. The ground we stand on is made of sand and time. The body dancing bones, donated, the home consumed. We beg for alms that are a temporary grace. Nothing separates us from the crazy lady, the wino in my father's new rags. We wander, and the shelter is the Sukkot bower that sun will wither and at night we see black space and faraway empty stars.

# A Letter to My Grandmother on Coming Home from Europe

## SARA PARETSKY

My grandmother came to America from eastern Europe in 1911, when she was not quite thirteen. Her father had been murdered in a pogrom in front of her, her mother, and her brothers and sisters. My grandmother had been too liberally educated; her mother was afraid the mob would turn on her next, and so she sent her eldest child, alone, to the new world.

My grandmother often talked about sailing into New York Harbor and seeing the Statue of Liberty, like a second mother, welcoming her under its outstretched arm. Her life was never easy. She never saw her mother or most of her family again: they perished in the Holocaust. Her education ended when she left Europe. She worked as a finisher in the garment industry for fifty cents a day, became active in the Garment Workers Union, became pregnant and married at fifteen. But she knew when she sailed in under the Statue that her life would not be in danger again because of who she was or what she thought or said. She had come home to freedom.

Immediately after the November, 2004 election, I was sent on a three-week speaking tour in Europe, in connection with a novel I wrote called *Blacklist*, which is set partly in the McCarthy era, and partly in the world of the patriot act. The book has won some important awards, but has also generated some vitriolic mail from people who accuse me of hating America and loving terrorists. When I walked into the U.S. consulate in Hamburg and saw a sketch of the Statue on the wall, I thought of my grandmother and broke down and wept.

Grannie, this is what we're doing now:

We imprisoned an artist in upstate New York for an installation piece he was creating around genetically modified food. When his wife died suddenly one morning and he called 911, the FBI arrived before the ambulance. He was arrested for having microorganisms in the apartment; he was held without charge until her autopsy was completed and showed that the benign, legally obtained organisms in his home had not caused her death. His trial, originally scheduled for this past January, keeps being postponed as the Justice Department tries to find grounds for his arrest, and in the mean time, his travel is restricted, and he is subject to frequent drug tests.

We arrested a library patron in Morristown, NJ, for looking at foreign-language pages on the Web. We held him for three days without charging him, without letting him call a lawyer, or notify his wife.

We arrested a man at St. John's College in Santa Fe, NM, for making a negative comment about George Bush in a chat room from the college library. We put a gag order on all the students and faculty, forbidding them to reveal that this arrest had taken place; the staff member who told me about it could be imprisoned for doing so.

We pressured a North Carolina Public Radio Station to drop a longtime sponsorship from a reproductive rights group, claiming that the FCC holds reproductive rights to be political and therefore not permissible donors.

We interrogated a California telephone repairman for criticizing George Bush; when the man said he thought there was freedom of speech in America, the FBI said there was, but they were still writing him up.

We've seized circulation and Internet-use records from at least 10 percent of the nation's libraries without showing probable cause.

We're imprisoning journalists for their coverage of a White House vendetta on a CIA agent; we coerced newspapers in Texas and Oregon to fire reporters who criticized the president's behavior in the days immediately after 9/11. We have held citizens and noncitizens alike for over three years in prison, without charging them, without giving them any idea on how long their incarceration might be, and we have "outsourced" their torture to Pakistan and Egypt.

When George Bush spoke at the Ohio State commencement in 2002, we threatened protestors with expulsion from the university.

We imprisoned an eighty-one-year-old Haitian Baptist minister when he landed at Miami airport on October 29, 2004, traveling with a valid passport and visa. We took away his blood pressure medicine and ridiculed him for not speaking clearly through his voice-box. He collapsed and died in our custody five days later.

In Germany, where people refer to themselves ironically as "old Europeans," there was a feeling of terrible loss and betrayal in the wake of the presidential election. People in their sixties told me that growing up in postwar Germany, they idealized America. Even when our faults were obvious, as they were with lynch mobs and segregation, these Germans saw America as struggling to become true to our ideals of justice and equality. Now, as Germans see the many ways in which we are turning our backs on those ideals in the name of protecting ourselves from terror, they feel a betrayal deeper than the loss of a lover. They fear, too, that as America moves the definition of radicalism to new points on a right-wing compass, other nations will follow suit. They fear that in a world without a beacon of liberty, there will be no curbs on totalitarian behavior anywhere.

Unlike our treatment of the French—I learned that French government employees in America still get several dozen hate letters a week—I never met any anti-American sentiment in Germany, despite the bewilderment that people feel. People were supportive and helpful, even if no one is very hopeful right now.

In Dresden, a man in his seventies said that anyone who thinks the worsening war in Iraq, and a worsening U.S. economy, would turn Americans against this administration, should look to Germany. He said he remembers the Second World War vividly, when people were willing to shed the last drop of their blood for a regime that had destroyed their economy while plunging them into a senseless war.

In Munich, the consul lectured the audience on how America is the oldest democracy in the world, and the fact that I was allowed to say things at odds with our government's official position was proof that free speech was alive and well in the country. He walked out in the middle of my remarks, when I was explaining that the State Department had removed all of Dashiell Hammett's books from consular and embassy libraries, after Hammett refused to name names during the McCarthy witch hunts.

The consul in Frankfurt said between seventy-five and a hundred twenty casualties from Iraq are flown in every week to the military hospital there, but we aren't allowed to see these wounded on television, nor are we allowed to see the coffins of our dead. The FCC pressured ABC television not to show *Saving Private Ryan* on Veterans Day—the movie's view of war is obscene, and showing it could have resulted in heavy penalties to the network.

In London, a mother of a four year old told me they had to stop watching television news; their daughter wanted to know why women in Iraq were putting their children into holes in the ground. "Do their mommies do it to keep them safe?" she asked.

My taxi driver to the Frankfurt airport was an Iranian refugee; he had served in the Iranian army during the Iran-Iraq War, and had lost his mother and both grandmothers. "Doesn't Mr. Bush know that in a war only the innocent suffer?" he asked, adding that he is a devout Muslim who fled Iran to protect himself and his wife from state-imposed religious and moral standards. "Why does America want to rule by religion?" he asked. "Religion makes a cruel government."

On the plane coming home, I sat next to an Englishman, urbane, fluent in four languages, traveling every month to South America or the Pacific Rim, who told me "you Yanks" had done the right thing in giving Bush four more years. "He's protecting you from terror," the man explained.

I told him about the imprisoned artist in upstate New York, and the other arrests and interrogations of writers, artists, ordinary citizens.

He paused for a minute, then said, "You Yanks put a lot of your people in prison, anyway."

I was bewildered, and asked if the fact that we do incarcerate a large percent of the population meant it was okay to arrest all our writers and artists.

"No," he said, "but it's a necessary price to pay for protection against terrorism. You'll be glad ten years from now that you did it."

Grannie, you know that's what a lot of people said in Germany in the 1930s—that the torture of Jews, communists, homosexuals, and the mentally retarded was a necessary price to pay for moving Germany in a better direction.

When I think of you sailing into New York Harbor alone, terrified, and seeing "the Mother of Exiles" lift her lamp beside the golden door, I feel my heart breaking.

> Not like the brazen giant of Greek fame,
> With conquering limbs astride from land to land;
> Here at our sea-washed, sunset gates shall stand
> A mighty woman with a torch, whose flame
> Is the imprisoned lightning, and her name
> Mother of Exiles. From her beacon-hand
> Glows world-wide welcome; her mild eyes command
> The air-bridged harbor that twin cities frame.
> "Keep ancient lands, your storied pomp!" cries she
> with silent lips. "Give me your tired, your poor,
> Your huddled masses yearning to breathe free,
> The wretched refuse of your teeming shore.
> Send these, the homeless, tempest-tost to me,
> I lift my lamp beside the golden door!"

# Marked by Carnival

## Dina Rubina

*Translated from the Russian by Daniel M. Jaffe*

The difference between the comic side of things and their cosmic side turns upon a single whistling consonant.

—V. V. Nabokov

For how many years have I been trying to understand what keeps me afloat in my not quite flawless, not quite painless, not quite cloudless existence here? I think—its unconcealed, brutal, murderous carnivalesque nature. The interchanging of faces, appearances, and masks; the topsy-turvy, inside-out sense of existence; the twisted situations, their blatant theatricality and blatant farcical idiocy. Masks that are daubed on crudely, a servant dressed up as lady, a lady—as courtesan, and everyone performing somebody else's role. They perform in crude, overly simplistic, hackneyed ways, for there's nothing you can do; it's burlesque.

And only on occasion does an attentive and mocking glance of the sort looking down at us from Velàzquez's portraits of jesters, flash through the eye slits of some idiotic mask.

Here's one such story.

In Israel there's a man with the surname of Lensky. This is not yet the carnival's beginning, not yet funny. A standard Jewish surname—even Pushkins turn up among our people.

At one time in the Soviet Union, this Lensky, as a sign of protest against the entry of Soviet tanks into Prague, burned a red flag on Riga's Freedom Square. Of course he was seized, tried, and given a sentence, which he served down to the last millisecond.

Afterward he repatriated to Israel, to his historic Homeland, to a democratic state where, he assumed, one could forget the dreadful communist dream.

But in Israel at that time the Labor Party was manning the helm, and as is well known, the national white-and-blue flag stood on one side of their rostrum while on the other—a red flag.

What's there to say? Lensky burned a red flag on Kings of Israel Square in Tel Aviv. He was seized, tried, and given a sentence (one must do justice—a much shorter one); he served it, then went free.

And he went off into Israeli freedom a hardened dissident.

He lived in the so-called Territories, became a member of Kach, walked around with a gun, participated in every antigovernment demonstration (regardless of which party was in power), and also rallied at every rally. He participated in every strike—be it of Ben Gurion Airport employees, or kindergarten and day care workers. In a word, a man sewn into the carnival costume of "the inveterate delinquent."

Need one even bother mentioning that the Israeli police and organs of state security became accustomed, at the least little hint of trouble, to tugging on the thread that would lead them to Lensky, the eternal dissident?

So here you go—my neighbor, working as some kind of low-level secretary in the investigations department of the Jerusalem police station, described a scene to me that she happened to witness the other day.

The characters:

A student, a youth about twenty, from a Leningrad intelligentsia family, brought to the country at age sixteen—that is, a person burdened by a moderate load of Russian culture.

A police officer, a Yemenite Jew about forty-five years old, brought to the country in childhood. In any case, not burdened by any load of Russian culture whatsoever.

The following dialogue took place between them:

Policeman: "Have you heard of Lensky?"

Student: "Yes . . . of course."

Policeman: "From whom?"

The student raised his brows ironically, glanced over at the secretary, finally said: "What exactly do you mean—from whom? From Pushkin."

The officer quickly jotted something down on the form in front of him. "And where is he now—do you know?"

"How do you mean—where?" the young man asked, on his guard. "C'mon . . . after all, they killed him . . ."

"What are you saying—they killed him!?" he cried out opposite. "Who killed him?!" He jumped up from behind his desk and started circling the room in a state of terrible agitation. Apparently, he was severely offended by the fact that this snot-nosed kid knew about Lensky's murder, whereas for some reason he, a police officer, did not. He stopped in front of the student and repeated: "Who killed him?"

The student, already sensing that this strange conversation with an insane fan of Pushkin's novel had taken some sort of wrong turn, shrank a bit and quietly said: "Why, of course . . . why, that . . . very Onegin . . ."

The policeman bolted over to his desk, quickly wrote down this testimony as well.

And only when he tried to clarify the exact date of the murder, and the youth, evidently calculating something in his mind, muttered that it was approximately in the first quarter of the nineteenth century . . . that there followed, as in Gogol—a final scene with bug-eyed figures standing in frozen stupefaction.

Our very language—an extremely important, if not the primary, substance of our existence in society's consciousness—is subjected to grotesque transformation, distortion, transfiguration of ordinary sense.

Pay attention: the manglings of language—comic linguistic situations—now occupy a huge place in the pages of humor publications everywhere in the emigration—in Germany, the USA, Israel.

The torturesome wearing of another's language, the gradual dressing up of one's consciousness—is it not a tragic, carnivalesque process, the essence of sickly émigré transfigurations?

For after all, as years pass, a coating of one's native language takes place as well, a partial losing of it, a lapsing of precise shadings, subtextual nuances.

The other day I was sitting in my publisher's office, discussing the terms of a new book's publication. The Russian radio, which broadcasts here twenty-four hours a day, was turned up full blast. The program was one which usually familiarizes listeners with this or that publication, which conducts interviews with famous journalists and writers, newspaper and magazine editors. An energetic, longtime resident hosts the program. The owner of a rich velvety baritone—at some point in his distant youth, he had recorded for the Leningrad subway lines ("Caution! The doors are closing; next station—Vasileostrovskaya"). After repatriating, he discovered that they had not yet constructed any subways here; however, the Voice of Israel radio station was looking for an announcer. At the beginning of the Great Aliyah, he flourished, started doing literary programs, interviews with visiting and local luminaries. True, in recent years his language didn't exactly get rusty as much as . . . he stopped listening to the sense of what he was saying.

We'll call his guest—editor-in-chief of a newspaper put out in Hebrew—Shapiro. In his suckling youth he was brought here from Russia, and he understands Russian, makes an effort to speak it, and sincerely believes that he knows this language his parents used to speak to him. Should one even bother clarifying that many of his words and phrases are, in fact, in need of supplemental clarification?

And so, right there on the public airwaves, the following dialogue took place:

"Mr. Shapiro," the host cheerily and energetically started off, "many in our radio audience are interested in knowing: How large is your venerable organ?" (It goes without saying that he had in mind the phrases: organs of government, organs of State security, organs of the press.)

Mr. Shapiro, a professor, the author of several monographs, the esteemed member of several foreign academies, became pensive for a moment, then, inflated with dignity, uttered slowly: "Of typical size. Normal. On Fridays it expands a little." (It goes without saying that he had in mind a number of his newspaper's Friday supplements.)

And neither of these gentlemen, each so highly pleased with himself, had the least inkling of what they were putting out on the public airwaves.

In this topsy-turvy, inside-out world our children are another matter altogether. It's understood that we brought them here for: a healthy sense of ethnic pride; a feeling of personal dignity; the ability to live unfettered; a knowledge of their ancestral language, traditions, culture, religion. However—my God!—not so that they could lose our sickly beloved, native, most-beautiful-in-the-world Russian language! But they, our children, are losing it at a catastrophic pace.

To force my twelve-year-old daughter to read a few pages of Russian is a minor's back-breaking labor, hacking one's pick axe through bedrock.

"So read *The Three Musketeers!*"

"I already read it in Hebrew."

"All right then, but the novel *Twenty Years After* hasn't been translated into Hebrew yet. It so happens, you don't know French, so, what—you're not going to read the novel at all? And do you know how many wonderful books have not yet been translated into Hebrew, but have already been translated into Russian? Are you content never to get to know them at all? And are you also going to read your own mother's books in Hebrew?"

Et cetera, et cetera.

And with impotent bitterness you observe your child slowly and inevitably swimming away to the shores of another language, and in horror you understand that she's not interested in the books of your beloved Yuri Koval, that your child has already read about Mary Poppins and Winnie the Pooh in Hebrew, and won't ever read in Russian.

An announcement on the doors of a bookstore: "Preserve Your Children's Language!!"

Two years in a row, I undertook nearly heroic efforts in this regard. For example, I sent my daughter to Russian language and literature lessons at a Russian night school. After class, she'd try, in an ingratiating tone, to discuss what she'd learned.

"So . . . What did you learn today?"

"That . . . you know . . . Tolstee."

"Lev Nikolaevich Tolstoy!" I said, articulating with exaggeration. "A great Russian writer. What exactly did you read?"

"That . . . 'The Plum Stern.' "

" 'Stone'!" I piped in with an exaggerated sigh. "It's a delightful story for children." A little boy, Vanya, steals and eats a plum from the dish on the family table, and later denies having done so. So as to trick him into admitting his crime, his father warns that if anyone swallowed the plum's pit, he'll surely die. Vanya suddenly exclaims that he didn't swallow the pit, just threw it out the window. "And can you tell me what happened in the story?" I asked my daughter.

She pondered, whimpered a little, shifted from foot to foot and looked toward the television where the popular comedy show *Zeh and Zeh!* was about to start (it's impossible to translate this exclamation precisely, it's approximately: "Oh, it's that!" or more precisely: "That's exactly it!"). The actors are rather burly men dressed up as women (huge false tits, disheveled wigs, vulgarly painted lips), who run around after one another wagging their behinds, who fall on the floor, hefting up their hairy legs in women's size 15 shoes, and who pinch each other's every conceivable body part.

For a long time, this political show elicited nothing besides bewilderment and loathing in me. Until I suddenly understood: it's actually nothing other than burlesque, carnival in its purest form!

"If you tell me the story of 'The Stone,' " I said, understanding the fully pathetic nature of this pedagogical device, "I'll let you turn on the television."

She thought for a long time, wrinkled her forehead, picked at a scab on her arm and, twisting her elbow, finally said: "Basically, they raised a ruckus because of some fruit... Imagine, they counted how much everyone ate! And the dad said to the children: 'My children! Either you ate this plum or you want to get something good out of it? To say nothing at all about completely dying...?' "

"You may turn on the television," I said with a falling voice.

Of course she can't even be bothered with "Let's have a little chat, Mama!" We'll be lucky if, in our old age she gives us maybe a glass of water, I say to my husband, if by that time she hasn't forgotten what "water" is in Russian...

It's curious that each of the otherworldly, other-homelandish, other-cultural phenomena that ended up here, in this infernally carnivalesque milieu, quickly draws itself into the furious whirlpool. You look—now here, now there, you catch a glimpse of a new mask in a mad dash, shaking loose for an instant from the dance circle that welcomed it and—here you go, a former engineer from Kuibishev is already tearing among colonnades of the Kardo's ancient Roman streets, basting a Russian tour guide's suit, for example, onto his back. He runs, waves a stick tied at the end with a bright rag, and cries: "The Vinnitsa Group, don't dilly-dally!"

By the way, enchanting stories develop in the Russian tour-leading field, ones literally stuffed with misunderstandings.

An acquaintance of mine, a tour guide, recently led a group of tourists from Baku along the "Jewish Jerusalem" route. Throughout the entire tour, a half-deaf old fellow underfoot kept getting muddled, listening while sticking out his big gray ear with a cupped palm.

Standing at the Wailing Wall, the tour guide said that after the Holocaust befell European Jewry, an explosion of national consciousness took place, and Jews proclaimed the independence of Israel.

After the tour, the old fellow went up to my acquaintance and, evidently agitated, asked in a monstrous accent: "Listen, pal, I don't get it: What sort of holocaust, what sort of explosion?"

The other patiently explained in a louder voice, that after the loss of six million Jews customarily referred to as the Holocaust, an explosion of na-tion-al con-scious-ness took place, and Jews proclaimed a State.

The old fellow sighed in tremendous relief, gave a smile and said: "Oh, thank God! I thought—Pompei!"

By the way: the costume of the *hamsin*-marked, half-undressed tourist and his mask with its painted-on, dazed expression of "God, it's broiling here!" is a phenomenon that has been spreading in recent years like the fall of the iron curtain.

So as to get a glimpse of Israel, a guest visited a friend of mine, their in-law, Vladimir Ivanovich, as it happens, a Candidate of Chemical Sciences. He arrived, stripped to his shorts (ours is, after all, a rather hot climate), and took to pacing around the apartment, hammering out, with palms on his naked belly, Mozart's "Turkish Rondeau."

One day went by that way, two, a week passed . . . Finally, the household, having gone nuts from the "Turkish Rondeau" already, decided to get this jackhammerer out of the house, if only for a day, by a surefire means: they bought him a ticket for the tour "Jerusalem—City of Three Religions."

They were living outside Haifa, and the tour bus was to set off from the central bus station. So, they explained to the in-law how to get to the bus station, sketched out where and how; they just forgot to write down the name of the tour. And he, while trying to get there, forgot which city he was going to, remembered only that it was the capital. So he went along the streets looking for Russian-speaking folk (not so hard to find), and came across a fresh little repatriate, asked her: "And could you tell me, Dear Citizeness, which city is the capital here?"

And that fool answered—what?: The correct answer is Tel Aviv. As they had taught her in Soviet school, "beware the long arm of Tel Aviv."

So, in-law Valdimir Ivanovich went looking for a bus that would take the route "Tel Aviv—City of Three Religions," which sounds so funny to the local ear that you could bust a gut laughing.

An aside about religions.

I'm not talking about the interrelations of the three great religions that huddle together on the holy Mt. of Olives square-inch. I'm talking about the opposition, discords, and antagonism within each of them. For within every confession we have, there are offshoots, inner circles and movements—a multitude! The Orthodox Church alone is divided here into White and Red, churches mortally at odds with one another. And the Catholics, and Protestants, and the Armenian and Georgian eparchies! And the Lutherans! And "Christians for Israel," annually organizing completely carnivalesque processions around Jerusalem! And . . . Christian Easter with reinforced contingents of Israeli police assembled on the square outside the Church of the Holy Sepulchre, Easter with the annual bloody brawls between brothers in Christ belonging to different movements of Christianity—now that's a carnival to end all carnivals!

In Jerusalem there's a little restaurant, Kangeroo. It's run by Lina and Dato—she's a Georgian Jew and he's a genuine Georgian, a devout Christian, a longtime secretary of the Patriarch of the

Georgian Orthodox Church. Former Russian nationals love it there: pleasant hosts, delicious cuisine, and one's own crowd, to boot.

One day the artist Sasha Okun brought to Kangeroo his guest from Italy, Father Sergio, a Jesuit. Here you go, he said, let me introduce you, this is Father Sergio. A Jesuit.

Dato, who, even under ordinary circumstances looks like a cat that's arched his back, totally bristled, took Sashka aside and hissed: "What's with you! How dare you bring a Jesuit into my home! You can't let them so much as darken your doorstep. In Switzerland, for example, they don't let them in at all, there's even a law!"

Nevertheless, innate Georgian hospitality apparently did not permit him to chase his guest away. They settled in at a table, ordered wine, *satsivi*, *lobiya*...

And Father Sergio, who, what's more, turned out to be a proponent of ecumenism, sat, enjoyed his food, eased back and gave a discourse as to how fine the world will be when all faiths become as one together in love.

Dato listened and listened, quietly started to boil. "Sergio, tell me," he finally asked suggestively. "When absolutely everybody finally becomes as one, who'll be on top?"

Father Sergio, a Jesuit after all, sensing a test, tented palms together beneath his chin, raised his eyes and humbly uttered: "God will be on top."

And there was nothing left for Dato to do but repeat the gesture. For several seconds they sat opposite one another like two parishioners of a single parish.

They remained silent... The refectory resumed.

"Sergio, tell me," Dato again started in suggestively, "when absolutely everybody becomes as one, who'll be just below God?"

"The Pope," the Jesuit answered meekly.

"Ne-ev-er!!" cried Dato, his eyes flashing.

They fell silent... A fresh plate of vegetables was brought out from the kitchen, young potatoes with salted cukes...

"Sergio, tell me," Dato again started in, "when absolutely everybody becomes as one, at the very absolute bottom, who'll be underneath everybody?"

"I will," said the Jesuit, smiling.

"No, I will!!" the Georgian exclaimed passionately, banging his fist on the table.

However, given that not all faiths have yet become as one in an upsurge of love with a common summit and with our dear Dato as common cornerstone foundation, it so happens that bloody fountains keep gushing in our public squares. After all, this too is in keeping with a Mediterranean carnival—take any Italian or Spanish medieval story: beneath the thunder of music and peals of laughter, amid passionate flare-ups, scores were forever being settled with an unfaithful paramour, a brute, a perfidious friend, a base traitor...

It's only our Near Eastern mincing-machine that has introduced something new into the history of the primordial Arab-Israeli carnival: when children—who are guilty of nothing, who have betrayed no one, who have never acted treacherously—explode into the air...

I returned home from the city. My son, all worked up, cried out to me: "Where've you been wandering around; we're going out of our minds here?!"

On television, they were broadcasting a special edition of the news: twenty minutes ago in downtown Jerusalem, on the pedestrian street of Ben Yehuda (in one of the stores where, an hour before, I'd bought myself a terrific day-planner in leather binding), three suicide terrorists blew themselves up. According to preliminary data, they'd been dressed up in women's clothes and had been strolling among café chairs set out on the street at this intoxicating hour of early evening coolness. There were many wounded, more than a dozen killed, among them—women, children...

On the television screen beneath the wail of ambulances, orderlies rushed about with stretchers, policemen ran around, people's faces flashed—twisted in horror, stone-cold from shock, overflowing with tears...

I pictured three madmen putting on enormous brassieres so as to fit as many explosives as possible, fastening on wigs, putting on women's shoes, painting their faces with lipstick—three madmen preparing themselves for the last carnival of their lives, simply glad for the chance to kill another dozen Jews. I tried to picture them changing clothes, looking at each other—wasn't it frightful fun, wasn't it funny, wasn't it impossible not to burst out laughing?!!

I hurled my purse—with the terrific new day-planner, which at any moment might cease coming in handy during this lifetime—into a corner. And I bellowed: "Good Lord, e-nough al-read-y!! Good Lord, enough of this nightmarish carnival! Good Lord, what to wear, how to dress up in disguise so as to become invisible, unassailable, invulnerable! Good Lord, how to disguise my children, all those close to me, the entire nation, so as to stop being an eternal target!!"

The next morning, after a sleepless night, I forbade the household from turning on the television or radio. I didn't want to hear anything, not a single detail about yesterday's act of terrorism, not a single name; I didn't want to see a single photograph of the victims. I was all squeezed out like a lemon, exhausted, I lacked the strength not only to work—but simply to live, move, engage in any routine activity whatsoever.

Shuffling slowly to the kitchen in my slippers, in total silence I brewed myself coffee and heard, almost stealthily, so as not to irritate me, my husband going out for a newspaper, and then quietly rustling pages in the living room.

Suddenly—I couldn't possibly be hearing right—his nearly hysterical laughter.

"A typo!" he cried out to me. "What a typo!"

And he showed me in the Classifieds section: "A Cain with much experience offers his services to perform circumcisions."

Of course; why not. Instead of setting "cohen," a descendant of the ancient priestly clan, the typesetter—probably a new repatriate—chose a word she better understood—"Cain," which instantly inserted itself as a new element in the eternal, impossible, unstoppable-for-a-single-minute, tragically splendid carnival.

# Homesick

## Else Lasker-Schüler

*Translated from the German by Janine Canan*

I cannot speak the language
of this cool country
or walk its pace.

Even the fleeting clouds
I cannot interpret.

Night is a step-queen.

Forever I must remember pharaoh's forests,
kiss the image of my stars.

My lips sparkle brightly
and tell of faraway.

I am a colorful picture book
open on your lap.

But your face spins
a veil of weeping.

Out of my glittering birds
the corals were gouged.

On the garden bushes
their soft nests turned to stone.

Who will anoint my dead palaces
that held the crowns of ancestors,
whose prayers sank in the holy stream.

# Memories of My Chinese Home

## Eve Perkal

My parents and I had survived almost three years in a ghetto in Shanghai, China. We had been forced to move, by a set date, into a section of Shanghai called Hongkew. This neighborhood was a far cry from the rather posh international settlement of the city; it was in a poor, outlying area, populated by lower-class tradesmen and coolies. Under the tutelage of their German allies, the Imperial Japanese occupation forces imposed such restrictive and primitive living arrangements on about 25,000 Central European Jewish refugees.

But how in the world did we wind up in Shanghai during World War II?

During the fateful summer of 1939, my parents and I were living in a furnished, two-room apartment in the Free City of Danzig, now called Gdansk. Our beautiful, spacious ten-room apartment, which also housed my father's medical practice, had been dissolved earlier because he was no longer permitted to practice medicine. All our furnishings had been sold, including my many toys; the packers had put all our household goods into two large crates.

We moved into a much smaller apartment, and my parents began the process of trying to immigrate to the United States. They had received an affidavit from a friend in Houston, and we had all passed the medical examination required for the immigration, and were waiting for the visa to America. Other family members had already left Danzig for Copenhagen, London, Tel Aviv, and Warsaw.

Our lives depended on the American quota system. Unfortunately, under American immigration law, my father was considered Polish because the East Prussian town where he had been born at the end of the nineteenth century was ceded to Poland at the Treaty of Versailles. He was, therefore, subject to the Polish quota, which had long been filled. Both my mother and I could have left immediately because we were both born in Danzig, which had its own, separate quota. My mother did not want to leave my father behind, so they frantically looked for a way out.

In that summer of 1939, the only country in the world that would accept Jews without a visa was China. Thus it came about that on July 28, 1939, we left Danzig by train to Marseilles, where we would board a French steamer that would take us to Shanghai.

On the way there we docked for a day in Saigon and went ashore. When we returned to the ship we heard the news that the war had started; Germany had occupied the area known as the Danzig Corridor and had invaded Poland.

We eventually reached Shanghai, and my parents rented a small apartment in the International Settlement of the city. My father opened his medical practice, sharing the office with another physician, and I was enrolled in a British girls' school. We adjusted to our new surroundings and life was tolerable. Then came Pearl Harbor, and the Japanese Occupation Forces took over. The British and Americans were put in detention camps while the Central European refugees were required to move into the ghetto in Hongkew.

We had been fortunate to be able to rent our own living quarters and thus did not have to live in one of the communal housing projects, known as "Heime," provided by the Jewish Committee, whereas less fortunate refugees had only a bed and small space to store their belongings, with virtually no privacy.

Our "palatial" accommodations, located in the rear of a building and up a flight of rickety, wooden stairs, were situated in a typical crowded lane, teeming with Chinese families. We had one room, measuring nine square meters—a nine-by-twelve rug would have been too large for it. It had a cement floor, and two windows next to each other that did not close properly. The electrical meter for the house was between the windows. That is why these rooms were called the "meter rooms."

The room housed an abundance of vermin that we constantly tried to eradicate, but it seemed that they had set up permanent residence in the innards of the small, straw-filled couch that served as my father's bed at night, and as the family sofa during the day. This couch stood along the wall between the windows and the door into our domicile. There was just enough space between the couch and the door for a narrow, white, wooden cabinet with glass doors that housed my father's few remaining medical instruments and pharmaceuticals.

On the opposite wall stood a small icebox, large enough to hold one block of ice, which, in the tropical summer months, enabled us to keep some of our food in edible condition. Next to it stood a double-door buffet cabinet, which contained dishes, cooking utensils, and a few staple food items. Along the wall across from the windows stood a wardrobe that started at the entrance door and extended to within a little more than four feet from the other wall. This area was blocked off with a green curtain. Centered between the two windows stood a small, square table with two chairs pushed against it. When we ate, my dad would sit on the couch with the table pushed up to him, and mother and I would sit on the two chairs.

And what was behind that mysterious, green curtain in the corner, next to the wardrobe? Two folded camping cots that were my mother's and my beds. Next to this stood the commode, a wooden, lidded bucket—our very own, nonflushable, waterless WC! The only water available to us—and this was only cold water, of course—was from a faucet downstairs in the entrance to the house, and it had to be carried up in a pail. The contents of the wooden bucket were collected every morning when they were dumped into a large cart. Our Chinese neighbors would bring their buckets outside and then clean them in the lane, but we paid the coolie who pulled his cart from house to house a weekly fee so that he would come upstairs to

Memories of My Chinese Home  ❖  85

our room to pick it up, clean it downstairs, and then bring it back up. We even became accustomed to the stench that heralded the approaching cart....

At night the table was turned upside down and placed on top of the icebox, with the two chairs stacked on top of it. The two camp cots were set up along side of father's couch. I had to get onto my cot before mother could set up hers, flush against mine; then there was about a foot of space between her cot and the buffet. We were a very close family....

The family meals were cooked on a small, hibachi-type charcoal brazier—we referred to it as the flowerpot—that stood on the stair landing just outside of our door. We had to light it outside of the house, and then, when the coals were glowing, carry it upstairs to the landing. We ate mostly one-course meals. Sometimes, though, we cooked rice or potatoes first and then wrapped the pot in which they were cooked in blankets and stored it underneath the bed pillows on the couch so it would stay warm until the other course was cooked and ready to be served. We never had more than two courses.

Winters were dreadfully cold. I remember dressing in additional garments when I went to bed because my canvas cot was just inches above the frigid, concrete floor. An old, woolen ski cap pulled over the ears helped protect me from the arctic draft from the windows. I suffered from frostbite, and all my toes were painfully cracked open so that I was unable to wear my shoes and had to shuffle about in a pair of crocheted slippers. One afternoon, frozen to the core, I dragged in the little hibachi stove, which stood outside our door on the little landing, still full of glowing coals, and placed it underneath the table, hoping to warm my feet. Fortunately, my parents returned before I was totally asphyxiated by the fumes.

I recall stifling, tropical summers where the only refreshment was some cold water, which, after it had been boiled and filled into empty bottles, had been cooled by lying on the one block of ice we would purchase from the itinerant iceman for our little, old icebox.

What a conversation piece this decrepit little piece of furniture would make today in someone's family room!

Meanwhile, the overall situation was worsening. Even the use of water was curtailed at certain times of the day, and this meant taking a bucket with a rope attached and fetching water from one of several wells in the lane. Thus we could take some sponge baths and get some slight relief from the itching of the prickly heat rash that afflicted all of us.

Our Japanese masters announced the possibility of air attacks and demanded that we immediately seal off our windows so that not the slightest flicker of light would be visible by enemy aircraft. Noncompliance would be punishable with incarceration. The Pao Chia, an auxiliary, "volunteer" force of refugees, would patrol the streets and report any violators. So, up went the blankets, secured with safety pins hooked to the nails in the window frames.

Life continued and conditions worsened. Most of our Chinese neighbors took their families and moved to the country. We had to remain behind in the almost deserted lanes awaiting the daily air attacks by the Americans. There were no air raid shelters, no protection. There was an electricity shortage; it would only be available for two hours in midday and again in the evening.

And then, finally, hopelessness gave way to joy: the war was over and we were free to walk beyond the ghetto boundaries. We encountered the first American sailors who, like playful children, ran up and down the waterfront, pulling the rickshaws while the coolies looked on uncomprehending—what were those white devils doing? The colonial way of life had come to its end.

Through the largesse of the U.S. Army, and the United Nations Relief and Rehabilitation Administration, we received C and K rations that spelled manna from heaven to us. We received our first carton from the UNRRA and eagerly ripped it open to look at its contents. One can had "fruit cocktail" written on it. My dad said that a cocktail was an alcoholic drink, and, always having been a devotee of the fruit of the vine and all other alcoholic beverages, he could hardly wait to get the tin opened. Imagine his disappointment to find a fruit compote with a bright, red cherry on top!

We found the canned ham with raisins unpalatable and gave it to the family cat that shared our living quarter in exchange for keeping it mouse and rat free. My favorite ration was the Hershey tropical chocolate bar. Almost two inches thick, solid as a rock, you really had to chew on this one, and, if the outside had turned a bit gray, it could be scraped off and the discoloration did not affect the taste.

Summer faded into fall, and with winter once more approaching, I was able to convince my parents that our room was large enough to accommodate a tiny stove. All we had to do was move the buffet a tiny bit toward the curtained corner to make enough room for it between the buffet and the icebox. The pipes could be vented through the upper corner of the window. But what would we use as fuel? C and K ration cartons, of course. We had saved them all, cut up and folded. We fed them into the belly of the little stove where they burned lustily, heating up the whole room, bringing a glow to our faces. And our future began to look as rosy as those dancing flames.

# II
# Place and Memory

❖

# To Return to One's Homeland

## Marjorie Agosin

*Translated from the Spanish by Betty Jean Craige*

To return to one's homeland
In the rainy season
When in the thick
Of the watchful forest
The winds
Converse with the locals
Who can read the tracks on land
The plumage of the birds
The passion of the silence
That hides voices behind the woodpile

To return to the south of Chile
In winter
To imagine the childhood
Of my mother in Osorno
To sense her face
In front of the windows
Opaque with frost and fog
To bind my voice with the river of her unquiet dreams

To arrive in Chile
In the rainy season
When ghosts scare away
The living
And the horses alone
Know the bitter wind
And the intruding rain
In the homes
Of the poor

To understand my country
Or what remains of it
For me
One must see it teetering
In the darkness
Hushed and long
Like southern nights
When women with translucent hands
Unacquainted with lace
Embroider their secrets in wool

To return to the south
And discover your body
That creased your pillows
In that house of stone
Where we were happy
At midnight
Awaiting lovely sorcerers
With eucalyptus tea

For even the most mysterious life
Holds nostalgia in a chrysalis
As if it were a love poem
To be read in the far south

On rainy nights
When the dead visit us
And peel away the covering
Of a dream

# Snow Unites Jerusalem

## Dalia Kaveh

*Translated from the Hebrew by Linda Stern Zisquit*

Snow unites Jerusalem,
such a fragile city.
Even the stone placed in it
cannot.

At Mt. Scopus
soldiers of a long-ago war
are suddenly returned home.
I too,
snow unites me
with my ancestors.

# From Cairo to Chicago

## Marcelle Levy

When the first Temple was destroyed in 586 BCE, Jews in exile established a community in Babylonia. After forty years many Jews returned to Israel. Others remained in Bazra, which became a thriving community with its own synagogues and yeshivot, a place where Jews could observe the Sabbath and celebrate Jewish holidays.

Before World War I, when Britain began to draft young men, many Jews who lived in Baghdad moved south to Bazra in order to avoid being drafted. That's how my grandparents ended up living in Bazra, then a small community where they had the freedom to live as Jews, practicing Jewish customs. Though some Jews later moved to other areas in order to earn a better living to support their families, both my parents were born in Bazra: my father, Ibrahim, was born there in 1896; my mother, Dina, in 1906. But it wasn't until Ibrahim and Dina were separately visiting their relatives in Egypt that they met one another and married. Together they had eight children and lived simply. My mother was a housewife and my father ran a fabric store in the town of Sohag, south of Cairo. It was very important to my parents that I attend a Jewish school in Cairo where I grew up. At El Sebil I learned some Hebrew, though Arabic and French were also taught.

Our family observed many Jewish traditions and celebrated all the holidays. Every Friday night we would sit together as a family while my mom would light Shabbat candles and my father would recite the blessings. Our Shabbat meal was fish, served either fried or baked, along with several meat dishes, cooked vegetables, and salad. For dessert we ate fresh fruit such as watermelon, cantaloupe, and grapes. During the week my mom would cook simple meals that might include chicken, spaghetti and meatballs, rice, vegetables, and dessert. Sometimes she would stuff phyllo dough with spinach and cheese, or make falafel from scratch. We also enjoyed hummus and eggplant dip with fresh pita bread.

On Jewish holidays such as Purim, my mother would prepare special dishes that she brought to neighbors and friends. Everyone enjoyed the huge assortment of cookies she'd bake, including butter cookies and mandelbread. For Passover, we prepared the table for our Seder. It took my father almost four hours to complete his reading of the Haggadah, during which he would sing and explain the meaning of the story to us. The long ceremony made us young children restless.

At the age of twenty I married my husband Elie and together we had three children, two boys and a girl. We also lived in Cairo, but not without pain. During the 1967 Six Day War, my husband and many other Jewish men were sent to concentration camps by the Egyptian government. The leather factory that my husband owned was confiscated and closed, its entire inventory depleted. My husband remained in the camp for over six months until I was able to get him out with the help of the French Embassy. He was sent to France where our entire family was united two weeks later. In November 1967, the Hebrew Immigrant Aid Society (HIAS) processed our papers and helped us on our journey to the United States.

We chose to go to the United States because my sister Jeannette and my brother Ralph who were already living in Chicago told us that life in America offered many opportunities, that it would be a great country in which to start over. On May 5, 1968, we arrived in Chicago and stayed temporarily in a hotel provided by HIAS. My husband found a job as a painter and I was still a housewife caring for young children.

A friend told me about Anshe Emet Synagogue and, because Jewish tradition is very important to us, we enrolled our children in Hebrew Day School there. After graduating from Anshe Emet, our children attended public high schools.

I am following in my mother's footsteps by continuing to cook some of the traditional foods she prepared: okra, stuffed onions and green peppers, stuffed zucchini, kobeba, musaka (eggplant and ground beef), chicken, meat, and fish. The desserts I prepare for my family include butter cookies, baklava, carrot cake, pound cake, and chocolate cake. Once in a while I even bake my own bread. We enjoy the aroma of these foods. On Jewish holidays I also cook traditional foods appropriate for the celebrations. By following in my mother's footsteps I am doing for my children what she did for me.

I am grateful to be living in America. All my children are working and successful. My husband has his own business and for the past thirty-three years I have worked for the Anshe Emet Day School. Our life in America has been good.

# Bella, 1908

## Ada Molinoff

Ellis Island
hard wood bench
I'm touched by the stranger
he searches for lice
pulls at my eyelids
pushes me back
barks his commands
I don't understand
*Ich nicht farsteyn*
I wait for America

bundle of cloth
worn-out green bag
strapped to my back
bread is all gone
no *kosher* food
water is all
David age three
clings to my knees
Harry he's one
so heavy to hold
Morris he's five
I clutch his left hand

endless
this wait for America

at last the release
the boat to the dock
Papa gets work
I scrub on my knees
we have two more *kinder*
Rose is so small
Bess cries all night
sometimes there's heat
we cook only rice
we wait for more work
how do I pray
here in America

David is taunted
fights neighborhood boys
Papa falls from a roof
he has to stay home
Harry leaves high school
he wanders the city
credit dries up
we ask for more time
winter comes early
we have only sweaters
how can we live
here in America

we move to Brooklyn
no more street brawls
here we have trees
Morris can study
David sells papers

Harry sweeps up
the girls go to school
how will they marry
*challah for Shabbos*
we light Mama's candles
my legs are in pain
here in America

the children grow up
they work in clean places
they move to the country
they try to come visit
they say I gave orders
I did what I had to
I saved our lives
the flight to America

their sons and their daughters
we mostly smile
eat little beauty
I give thanks to *Hashem*
*ess shayneh maideleh*
now that we can
warm noodle kugel
tender pot roast
strawberry soda
a glassful of tea
now we are here
at last in America

# Sisters

## Caroline Smadja

"I'd like to tell you about my life because..." I check my sister's face for fear of losing her before I begin. We sit across from each other in the back of a seedy *café-tabac*, on the frost-bit town square of a Parisian suburb. The corners of her small mouth move up imperceptibly, a sketch of a smile à la Mona Lisa only I can see because, though we've lived away from each other for over fifteen years, to the point of estrangement, her face was my daily landscape from birth to early adulthood. I had hundreds of minutes of silence like this one to decipher its modulations.

"I'd love to hear about your routine in San Francisco," she replies.

*My routine?* "What I want to say now goes much deeper." I struggle to find the right words to expose to her a twenty-five year old scar. "I need to tell you why I left Paris. Why I had to. I finally realized the essential reason for my leaving. I'm only now beginning to forgive Maman for something that in my unconscious I'd never forgiven her for."

I stop short at the sight of two smoking plates approaching. "*Deux omelettes-jambon-frites,*" the waiter announces. We begin to cut our food with our knives, the proper French way, rather than bending the fork sideways like most Americans do—which drives me crazy—to force it to do the job meant for a blade.

"There are things I'd buried inside for so long, I thought I was over them. But obviously, I never was. Never will be as long as I live. Our leaving for Israel, I mean, and the role *she* played in uprooting me from... Home. To this day, I don't know how you felt, we never talked about any of this."

My sister's eyes turn wistful but she continues to chew in silence.

"You never said anything, never protested. I felt so alone."

"I'd convinced myself I was happy as long as they were."

"Were you?"

"I didn't ask myself the question. As their older daughter, I saw it my duty not to make waves."

"What about the villa?"

"We'd already lost it."

"You're right. If it hadn't been for all her Zionist bullshit, I'd still be living there. I never would have left."

In the near-imperceptible softening of my sister's gaze, I can see my words have touched a nerve. She's found out something she didn't know minutes earlier.

"Papa feels the same," I continue. "Every time I mention the villa, his eyes sparkle. He talks of it with incredible nostalgia, as if it was the most special place on earth."

"It was!"

My sister and I speak in unison, like we used to long ago. At this moment, we both return to the big stone house perched on the hill, its front walls laced with jasmine and bougainvillea; to the wide verandah that encompassed all that the world had to offer: the red-tiled roofs and pine trees dotting the landscape of Nice, the *Baie des Anges* glittering on the horizon. We walk through the ticklish grass that was hardly ever mowed, hide behind the palm trees that cast shade over the Ping-Pong table, hold meetings at the fig tree that spread its branches and rough, finger-like leaves over the railing.

"He would never have left either," I say. "But he acted like a coward. That may be what I most resent. The way he wouldn't protect us."

"He couldn't protect his own self."

"True. In any case, once I'd been uprooted, not once but twice.... What am I saying? *Three* times. After all, we were uprooted a first time. From Tunisia."

"We were babies and they had no choice."

"I know, Jews weren't safe anymore. But I've long felt deprived of a past that was a birth right."

"I'd rather not go there, ever," she mutters.

"Precisely! Because your roots were yanked out before they could grow. You're scared of being disappointed."

"Which is why I've never returned to Nice. It'd be—"

"Too sad, yes. Reality could kill what you kept alive in here." I cover my left breast with the palm of my hand. "This reminds me: about a year ago, she sent me a photo of the villa, did I ever tell you?"

"No."

"Well, she went on some kind of pilgrimage. Don't ask why, since she's complained for years that it was as remote as a prison and all. I get a letter one day, with a picture of the villa, no prior warning or anything. The sight broke my heart. They'd given it some phony name like 'Il Campanile,' and they'd repainted the gate and railings a glossy black. Awful."

My sister falls into reverie, then asks: "Aqua, sort of?"

"Mint. But aqua's close enough," I reply. "Against the evil eye," I add with a little smile.

"I doubt that's what the landlord had in mind."

"It pleases me to think this. One look at that photo made me tear up. I hid it in a drawer. I wrote her how sad it made me. So she wrote back she had no idea it had pained me, almost reproaching me for not being happy to receive it."

"Typical," my sister says.

"I often feel my own mother has no clue who I am."

"You're probably right."

"I so wish she did."

"Forget it." Her voice is a mixture of sarcasm and pragmatism.

"To get back to why I moved to the U.S.: leaving was *my* choice at last, a kind of revenge. But I've become aware of this only recently. I didn't mean to punish them."

"You did."

"I often feel like you still resent me for this choice, as if you took it personally. You felt I abandoned you."

She doesn't need to reply. Her dark, sorrowful eyes say it all.

"There's more than one way to leave someone," I continue. It's something I've never dared tell her. "You always think geography, but you'd taken your distance long before I was physically gone. When Sophia lived with us, you had no more use for me, I became the third wheel."

She turns to the wall to avoid my eyes. "I realized years later that's how you must have felt," she mumbles.

It's her way of saying "I'm sorry." I expect nothing more. In fact, I had no expectation, just the need to voice a pain muzzled for nearly twenty years.

"In any case, it wasn't you I left, but a situation, a city I couldn't stand."

"You fled."

"No, I didn't! You've often said this, it's wrong. It was a well-thought out choice, the need to begin anew. Fleeing is an impulsive reaction. I could find no other option. I'd lost my landmarks, after we'd been"—I put my knife and fork on both sides of my plate and make a round gesture with my hands—"Dragged all over."

"Yes," she says emphatically. "As if we'd been nothing more than plastic bags."

"*Plastic bags?*"

"That's the image that came to me once we'd left Jerusalem and been taken here. That they treated us like plastic bags."

"Luggage, you mean?"

"Luggage has weight. We barely floated around, or rather behind them."

"Plastic bags," I repeat under my breath.

"That's how I felt the whole time but I realized it only in hindsight. Like I said earlier, I'd been taught to follow along."

"True, we were very docile—"

"You were a pest!"

"I barked but didn't bite. I had no power."

"Neither of us had any."

"I so wish you'd told me then what you're saying now."

Her no-comment look warns me she's about to fall silent.

"You didn't suffer too much then?" I ask, afraid her muteness might end the conversation.

"I focused on cramming for the *Bac*. Plus, I had less adjusting to do than you," she adds.

I roll my eyes. "I'll never forget that first day at *Beit Sefer Denmark*. I had no clue where the classroom was, I couldn't even ask my way around in Hebrew."

"I never wanted to be in your place."

"Me neither. I spent six months at a desk not understanding a damn thing."

"I'd have died of boredom."

"I killed time by sketching in the margins of my notebooks."

"Good thing you could draw."

"My classmates begged for their portraits at recess. They wouldn't leave me alone. You know how Israelis are? And our head teacher put me in charge of the Purim decoration." I smile at the memory, the rare sense of belonging this gave me. "Oddly, this ended up being my best school year ever."

"Same here. I mean, we worked like hell, but we had the time of our lives at the Lycée Français in Jerusalem!"

We exchange a faint smile.

"What kills me to this day though is that they haven't acknowledged anything. I've dropped hints but—"

"What did she say?"

" 'Water under the bridge.' Real insightful of a psychotherapist like her, *non*? Papa was even worse. The few times I broached the subject, he retorted—you know how he fires the bullet right back in your face—that I was insufferable, that I never gave Paris a try. I mean, there I was, forced to change schools four times in three years, tossed from Nice to Jerusalem, from Jerusalem to Paris. And we were supposed to grit our teeth and smile through it all? Foolish of me, I know, but I'm still hoping they'll apologize."

"Dream on!"

"Funny, we reacted like night and day. I became a wanderer and you, a potted plant."

We laugh. "Potted plant" is the term her husband found to mock her sedentary ways. My sister hasn't visited me in ten years—her first child was six months old then. She was a no show at my wedding, which still hurts me.

"That's the only way I feel safe."

"A train ride is enough to stress you out. It'd drive me crazy to live this way. I need to see the world or at least know I can. That's how I feel safe." I pause. "Saf*er*, in any case."

"I prefer to stay close to home."

"See, France ceased to be my home aeons ago. Once we moved to Paris, I lived in foreign territory."

"But you're French!"

"That's only what's written on my passport. As soon as I land here, I turn into an American tourist. I like it, actually. The only times I can enjoy Paris are when I have a return ticket to San Francisco."

"That's a little sad."

"*Eso es la vida, Carolina!*"

We grin at what's long become an inside joke. One of my classmates at the high school I attended in Jerusalem, an Argentinean immigrant named Gadi, used to tell me somberly "Such is life," in his native tongue whenever he could find no better explanation to why there were hardships in the world. He, who was barely older than I, sounded like a wise old man who'd seen it all.

We're ending with coffee. I ordered mine with extra water, American style.

"Do you know," I tell my sister, "I never talk about this part of my life?"

"Me neither."

"Not even to your children?"

"The little they heard is through Maman."

I nod. "It isn't out of wanting to hide it, it simply doesn't occur to me. It's too . . . "

"Yes!" she answers. And I know she's filled in the blanks with the words I mean—*private*, *painful*—as well as others that don't figure in the dictionary.

"To some extent, it's like these two years in Israel happened to someone else. They feel like a parenthesis, forever closed. And yet, they derailed my entire life."

It is my sister's turn to nod. As we slide out of the plastic booth and cover ourselves in layers against the winter cold, we both know this rare outing together also was a parenthesis. We'll go on living apart, she in a suburb of Paris, me in another hemisphere. Neither of us will bring up the subject again. As if the past had never existed. As if this lunch had not taken place.

Yet, what we shared is only ours.

# Jewish Oil Brat

## Davi Walders

imagine
*her*

looking through the dusty window,
sand cyclones swirling in the distance
above ten thousand men sleeping in tents,
the endless tracks of the Texas Southern
Pacific and a two-day honeymoon long past,
her eyes large above her swollen belly

imagine
*longhorns*

snorting at windows she tries to keep
clean, an elm so rare she waters it
growing through the warped floor,
sand hill cranes pecking at lizards
coiled in caleche pits, dogs slower
than armadillos crying in moonless nights

imagine
*fifteen*

miles from Big Spring, fifteen miles
from nowhere, fifteen frame cottages
resisting the wind, the Settles family
happy to lease to oil squatters
banking green between cactus and
cattle straggling along rutted roads

imagine
*fifty*

thousand fenced acres, the Conoco gates
opening for a skinny immigrant of a man,
his *shtetl* Yiddish buried in scholarships
and a deep Texas drawl, his brow already
creased from sun, breaking the rule of dusty
boots, the door slamming behind him

imagine
*the two*

of them, ignoring the spotless sky,
the worsening war, whirling through
sand, cactus, and rattlers, holding onto
each other in an old Studebaker, bouncing
by derricks pumping like mules and you,
a *sabra,*\* about to be born here

*imagine.*

---

\**Sabra: Cactus in Hebrew; used to describe the first generation born in Israel.*

# Shalom Bayit

## Davi Walders

To braid a *challah*
in a quiet house
is to work,
settling yeast
into water, salt
into flour, eggs
into dough,
separations yielding,
fingers sticky, sweet,
warm with morning
buoyancy

to braid a *challah*
in a quiet house
is to remember
a flecked recipe
beneath a window,
the path of four
hands kneading,
mother and child
back and forth
before and after,
again and again
blending

to braid a *challah*
in a quiet home
is to praise
small movements
of hand and eye
over, under,
weaving, crossing
small moments
twisting, waiting
watching the day
rise into golden
*shalom bayit*
*shalom bayit*

# All But My Life

## Gerda Weissmann Klein

When in September 1946, the wheels of the plane bringing Kurt, my husband, and me from Paris and London touched American soil, he tightened his arms around me and said simply, "You have come home." It has been home, better than I ever dreamed it would be. I love this country as only one who has been homeless for so long can understand. I love it with a possessive fierceness that excuses its inadequacies, because I deeply want to belong. And I am still fearful of rejection, feeling I have no right to criticize, only an obligation to help correct. I marvel at my three children's total acceptance of their birthright and rejoice in their good fortune.

The establishment of the State of Israel in 1948 helped me to become a better American. The pain and loss I experienced in Poland, the country of my birth, obliterated the nostalgic thoughts of a childhood home for which I yearn. I have found the answer to that longing in the tradition of my religion and in the land of my ancient ancestors. Israel, by extending the law of return to all Jews, has become the metaphorical sepulcher of my parents as well as my spiritual childhood home.

While my love for Israel represents my love for my parents and our shared past, the United States is my country of choice, my adult home. This country represents the love I harbor for my husband, my children, and my grandchildren. One complements the other; by being mutually supportive, they enrich and heal.

I fell in love with this country from the moment I first stepped upon its soil. It felt so right, so expansive, so free, so hospitable, and I desperately wanted to become part of the American mainstream.

I had envisioned Buffalo, which was to become my American home, as a utopian city beneath an ever-blue, brilliant sky, and had dismissed Paris, London, and New York, my way stations to this utopia. During the drive from the grand, imposing New York Central railroad station in Buffalo, I was confronted with my new city's small wooden houses, huddled together like refugees, but my disappointment lasted only a few moments. I was ready to love the city and willing to defend it, even to myself. My affection was not misplaced. Buffalo did become a true home. It nurtured me, and later my children played and laughed under rows of elm trees while I immersed myself in a new life.

In time we would move from our first apartment to another part of the city, but I would occasionally drive past the familiar location that held so much of our early memories. I would remember how it had seemed to me on my first night in Buffalo, and a picture would flash through my mind. Long after Kurt had fallen asleep, I roamed through the apartment's modest rooms, stopping at the refrigerator in the tiny kitchenette that Kurt's friends had amply stocked. I had always loved fruit, so I took out an apple; but before I could catch the door, it slammed shut with a bang, and terror seized me. How many years had it been since I had lived in a home where I could take whatever I wanted with impunity? It was all mine now: the apple and the refrigerator. I opened the door, fully intending to let it slam shut. Instead, I caught it in time, closed it gently, and, grateful, went to bed.

# Kentucky Fried Chicken

## Arlene Zide

I. It begins with
the gray challenge of squares
the chalked boxes ending in Blue Heaven
the snap of the rope
they don't let you cross.

You get your own rope
red-handled, tight
one day threaten the bully down the block.
Her mother comes running to tell,
your mother laughs—about time!

Cowering in a corner,
afraid to venture home,
you find the bigger, tough-looking black girls
from the Quonsets on the other side of Bruckner Boulevard
don't like bullies either. They
take your hand, lead you
from the schoolyard.

You learn
about sharp surfaces.

II. Sometimes you wander
along the dark
streets below the clatter of the El-tracks
past the bank on the corner, to the movies
where you plunk down your quarter for the Saturday morning
   twofers
double-feature, cartoons at the Ward theater
sneaking in
the carefully chosen nickel candy
from the candy store next door.

Sometimes all the way to the library
where you choose the week's
dream treasures.

Sometimes
dare to go beyond.
Thrill to the concrete playground
hang by your toes from the monkey bars
when your mother isn't looking.

Once even took your bike
and rode the narrow path along the expressway fence
    you'd watched your father
      on those Sunday family drives
all the way to the Bronx zoo
arrived just before closing, turned around and left right away—
skirting those two unshaven men
instinctively knowing
they didn't look like they were interested in the wild animals
but not really old enough to know why.

III. Today you stand with your thirty-year-old son
shanghaied into escorting you

through what is no longer a neighborhood of warm rolls,
  luncheonettes,
cranky old men *davening* in *shuls*, the genteel poor,
past the hated crawling cockroach house of your childhood,
grown oddly miniature,
drabber than you'd remembered,
not even space
for those fuchsia four-o'clocks
to soften the fence,
garbage cans
no longer chained where they once were.

Face pressed to the fence barring the Bruckner now–Expressway
staring across to PS 93, a shudder of recognition,
the taste of aversion
bitter on the tongue, heart seizing up
as you make out the same bleak schoolyard, not one tree and
three stories of rusted window-gratings,
the same
cold
dread.

You walk, arm hooked in his, beneath the El-tracks
the street seems
dirtier, rank,
water everywhere
reminding you of drainage
in India.
In the window of what once was Daitch's dairy
a sign hawks *pulpo*, octopus and shrimp
not pot cheese and man-size blocks of creamery butter,
unsalted and cut off at all angles in uneven chunks
the way your grandmother insisted.
The marquee now stars underwear in Spanish.

Kentucky Fried Chicken ❖ 121

Even the vegetables in the stands are different,
slightly exotic.

Only Manufacturer's Trust
is still Manufacturer's Trust.

IV. You thread
the familiar/unfamiliar landscape
your son delights in knowing
his mother's child
self, unfamiliar/familiar
wants to see where she sat eating garlic pizza
at Luigi's; disappointed, learns at the local *bodega*
that it closed
just a few years back.

You keep looking for the library.
Come from around the back, sight
its carved stones,
turn the corner and catch
lumps in the throat choking back
the sinking shock—
where once there had been books, the warmth of sunlit chairs and
    tables,
shelves and shelves
of books-slick
counters, the plastic
angled world
of Kentucky Fried Chicken.

You don't go in.

You ride back home
in silence, ghosts

and regret
set heavily,
finally
to rest.

# America

## Viva Hammer

I came to America on April 24, 1990, to New York City.

The Saturday after I arrived, a heat wave ignited the City. I pulled on a T-shirt and walked from my apartment on the Upper East Side all the way to the bottom of Manhattan. The streets were ablaze, with markets and street vendors, and every person in America out walking with me. I smiled as people stared at my front, on which was displayed a giant red image of Karl Marx, founder of communism, with his name in bold on top. Here was the center of everything he despised: individuality; people making money and keeping some of it; desperate poverty slumped on the doorstep of obscene wealth. I was walking down the broadway of capitalism with Marx on my front and there were none to make me afraid.

In the year or so before I left Sydney, Australia, it rained continuously, a pelting, torrential rain that enclosed each inhabitant in her own private storm. Most days I couldn't see two arms' lengths ahead of me; I moved from the library to my study and back, encased in moving gray walls. I designed my entire Law School program based on the New York bar exam requirements, and the resulting timetable was a patchwork of overlaps and conflicts. At an appointed time every week, I reached out to my contacts across the ocean, readying the soil for my arrival. I held my breath waiting for the *beep* of the international phone connection; each expensive call I justified as an investment in my future.

My parents' families arrived in Australia 100 years apart. In 1857, my mothers' Polish-born great-grandparents, Hannah and Philip Blashki, booked a passage from England to America. The night before the Blashkis were set to sail, they loaded their possessions onto the boat that was to take them to the New World. Alas, an "unexpected high tide" forced the captain to leave ahead of schedule, and so the young couple was left waiting at the dock, all their worldly goods on the high seas.

As compensation for this most unfortunate miscalculation, the shipping company offered the Blashkis passage to Australia. Apparently for lack of options, they accepted, and on the four-month trip, Hannah Blashki became pregnant with twins. They became the first Jewish boy twins born on Australian soil. Hannah bore twelve more children after that, perhaps deciding that she would single-handedly colonize the continent.

My father's arrival in Australia was no less serendipitous. After his family returned to their Hungarian town following the liberation of the Nazi camps, he tried many times to escape to Israel. But the communists policed their borders well, and he never made it beyond their watch. After the 1956 Hungarian Revolution, my father's family followed a brother who had come earlier to Sydney, just as that brother had followed an uncle who had come immediately after the war—a daisy chain of refugees.

Of his surviving siblings, only my father remained Jewishly observant after the War, and it was important for him that we, his children, attend religious day school. Yeshiva College was a decrepit affair, housed in condemned buildings, teachers coming and going on a monthly basis. But one *rebbe* captivated me, teaching the sing-song of Torah as he rocked back and forth, his red beard caressing the holy books. The intensity of his faith fed my spirit, and so I moved closer to tradition, shepherding my parents along with me.

The path my *rebbe* started me on I could not carry far in Australia. There were no places I could continue to study the wonderful texts I had discovered with him, and no peers to study with.

After high school, a little coterie of girls headed for Yeshiva study in Israel, and after we returned to Sydney, it was clear none of us would stay. Our neighborhood was like a way station, a place where young people checked in between their year in Israel and their next stopping point. Most intended to return to Israel, quickly completing their studies, attending the fervent youth minyanim, eyes only for Zion.

I could not see myself moving to Israel. The many contradictions in my soul: religious passion, feminism, professional ambition, would not, I thought, fit well in Israel's sharply divided society. I yearned for tolerance, and so I looked to pluralistic America.

There is a Hasidic idea that This World, of the flesh, is merely a *prozdor*, a corridor, to the World to Come, of the souls. Thus I felt about my stay in Australia, and no time more so than when I was in university, preparing myself for the leap to New York, my Destination. I studied furiously, blocking all distractions, directing my thoughts only to adapting my credentials on a foreign soil. Two days after I finished my final Law School exams, I was on a plane to New York, and immediately began preparing for the New York Bar.

I planned to stay with friends on my arrival in New York. Without a budget other than my parents' largesse, renting an apartment would have been an impossible luxury. What I didn't figure was that studying for the Bar while camping out in someone's living room might be impossible, particularly at times there were others also standing in line for my friends' free Manhattan accommodation. So I moved from couch to couch in various people's homes until I found something affordable in an elderly *rebbetzin*'s apartment in the Lower East Side. What I saved in money I paid for in abuse, and so as soon as the exams were over, I went back to staying with friends, never knowing each morning where I would spend the next night.

This itinerant arrangement, whereby I would stay with generous friends until they politely moved me on, lasted years. Through a long and difficult job hunt, and even after starting work, I carted all my worldly goods around with me from day to day, anticipating the next hasty move. I cannot fathom now how I managed this bizarre lifestyle, but I think that I was looking for a home, someplace to nest, and I needed to share with people who had already done their home-work, filling their spaces with permanence, with belonging.

Eventually, I did find an apartment; it was an illegal sublease from a single woman in her forties who was moving West. Her studio was crowded with things from the landlady's life, but I did not mind; I still needed that sense of prior habitation. The first day I turned the key on my apartment, I gasped. *Can money buy this?* I thought. *A place of my very own?* I grew into the space over the few months I lived there, learned to keep house, and host guests. I bought some things, not having to weigh the decision to purchase with the knowledge that I would have to carry the new goods with me every night.

It did not last long. The landlady decided she could not survive out of New York, and she gave me notice to leave. I was back with friends for a while, and then into another studio in the same complex as my first apartment. Having been homeless myself, I was very hospitable, and let unlimited numbers of people come and stay. The co-op board decided I was running a boardinghouse and threw me out of the second apartment within ten days of my occupying it (the landlord charged me a full month's rent, of course). But this time, I had a StairMaster to move with me, and needed help. Sometimes I search for things now that I know I owned at some point during this period, and when I cannot find them, I assume they must have fallen off one of the carts I used to move my possessions from one of those studios to the next.

The last studio I rented was emptier than the others, and initially, I enjoyed the blank walls and silence; I didn't even want a telephone. My life was so busy with work and committee meetings and dating, that I wanted some quiet when I came home at night. But my friends were outraged that I would be incommunicado for the few hours a day I was home, and I relented, buying a phone and even an answering machine in the end.

I had come to New York to experience everything, a goal I pursued relentlessly. Every Shabbat, I invited myself to another community. Any organization that had a purpose even remotely interesting, I volunteered for. And I dated all who came along. From divorced middle-aged Libertarians, to Hasidic foreign-currency dealers, I reveled in the possibilities.

People asked if I missed Australia, and invariably, I answered no. I spoke to my parents every day, told them about all the things that filled my life. I felt I had transported myself to a new place and kept my family close to me; there was nothing to miss.

Then I met my husband-to-be, and after a short period of dating and engagement, we were married. Into my cozy studio came 1,000 books, and another bed. We rented a second apartment, in Brooklyn, so that on weekends we could be close to the congregation where my husband was Rabbi. Our lives were split between these two spaces; it infuriated my husband, but I liked the variety.

After our daughter was born, we consolidated ourselves in Sheepshead Bay, an outlying neighborhood in Brooklyn, among anonymous neighbors, at the end of civilization. Through endlessly long nights of half-sleep, nursing my baby, I began to dream about Australia again. And the deeper I trek into the terrain of my children's childhood, the more vivid are the scenes of my own. There are curves of my birthplace that shape my thoughts more than the curves of my own body. The extreme hybrid colors of Sydney, matching teal blue sea and aqua green eucalyptus leaves are the beginnings of my palette. The soft grooves of my mind where I visit the beautiful places of my childhood are polluted up with the aesthetic of the harsh city in which I have made my adult home. I used to think that some things are so familiar, so often visited, that they can never be forgotten. I was wrong: there is nothing indelible in the human mind. I am trying to remember the contours of the journey to places I went every day; the order of the shops in the shopping strip near my home; where it was I changed buses to get to high school. I cannot remember anymore.

How can you forget your birthplace?

I return to Sydney less and less often now; it is such a difficult trip and all the more so with young children. When I return after these long intervals, everything is changed: Sydney is booming, and the lush greenery is being cut down to make space for elaborate concrete creations. My parents no longer live in the neighborhood where I spent my formative years, and the Jewish community has been transformed by a wave of South African immigrants.

What was home when I was young I cannot return to: the buildings have been demolished, the people are gone. What is home now is always temporary, as we anticipate the endless moves we will subject ourselves to. In the first ten years of marriage, my husband and I moved seven times, and neither of us feels attached to our current abode or community, even though we have been here a while now.

But as we continue to linger in this particular, random place, it occurs to me that its contours are being imprinted onto the minds of our children. Sometime hence, they will pull out from their memories images of the park at the bottom of our street, or the snowstorm that left a drift higher than their heads. The East Coast fall colors will be their first palettes, and the bumpy ride to school a journey they'll trace over in their heads.

This is home: a place you go in your mind (deep in the night) when you're alone and nothing is familiar.

# East

## Rochelle Mass

The house faced east. The architect intended fresh light
the first stream of morning. He placed long, wide windows
in the kitchen wall, was sure facing east would bring her
the spirit of Jerusalem, David's wisdom.

For her, east was keffiya'd* men at roadblocks unloading
chairs and carpets with plump women who squatted,
staring at their feet till officials ordered them to move on—
their green-and-white license plates eventually fading
in the dust.

She heard the muezzin from the village of Sandalah, just
over the hill, whining first prayers, watched Jenin, farther east
over the green line, fill the horizon with new homes and
brooding intentions.

*Head scarves, often with red-and-black checkered fabric, sometimes white, traditionally worn by Arab men.

# The Mah-Jongg Set

## Deborah Nodler Rosen

I am eight. My mother is beautiful. Mah-Jongg is my life—the place where my belonging to myself begins. I belong to a house, a sturdy red brick house in Philadelphia. I belong to two parents devoted to their (still) only child. And, because I belong to my parents, I belong to Judaism—to all those wise and righteous biblical heroes and heroines whose descendant I am, for Deborah, the judge and poet, for whom I am named.

By first grade I know my parents can walk down any street in the world, heads high, the probity of their lives as unquestioned as mother's beauty. The vigilance with which they guard their reputations and appearance so as to bring no shame on themselves or Judaism is a serious burden for a skinny little bucktoothed child to heft. How can I live up to the proper standards of "good" and "pretty" and "Jewish" when I do not even know the real-life judges whom my mother has picked to please or what they value. Too young or too stunned by these expectations, which always seem to exceed my abilities, mortification is often the air I breathe. My life seems a game of blindman's bluff as if, eyes covered by one of Mother's filmy scarves, I can't know who is pointing to me or why. I want to throw off all judgments the way I throw off my old pink robe when I am finished being sick.

That moment comes for me when I gather up the magical, mysterious Chinese ivory Mah-Jongg tiles and, exiled beneath the baby grand piano, build a gateless wall around myself—a fortress where I need not please, achieve, or use my time wisely. Inside my burnt-butter tiles I spend empty-headed hours arranging birds and flowers and deciphering the secret messages of the Chinese glyphs. Inside I am home safe. Inside I cannot fail, am "good enough" and free from time's relentless demands. Thoughts like motes of dust drift about my mind, collide and something new is born. I discover the joy of happenstance as I pick up tiles however they come to hand and make up words for them. I lay "cloud" next to "mirror" or "turtle" next to "princess" and reverie evolves into my own fairy tales. With a shiver I realize that out of nothing I have generated something—an idea, a story, a possession I can own or even offer as a gift. No wonder God made the world! Who can resist this delicious power of creation.

After I put the Mah-Jongg set away I still have my new observations and, in some magical transformation, they re-create me. The tiles have become language for me and within this language of tiles and words I am able to find myself. Home becomes the place where the stories are kept while I am busy attending to my moral, Jewish, good, and pretty daily life. The turtle carries his home on his back; I carried mine inside—a secret impenetrable Mah-Jongg fortress where I stored all imaginings. And they were good.

All these years later and a grandmother, I build Mah-Jongg castles and gardens with my grandchildren whenever they come to visit just as I did with their parents a generation before. We make up our own games and designs—never play by the rules, which I have steadfastly refused to learn. If I give these cherished children nothing else, I want to give them the permission and the joy to create.

Slowly I have come to realize that in my acute craving for a safe "home," I have instinctively re-created my fortress wall—this time with paint and thread, wood and beads. I have covered my walls with tapestries, paintings, and crafty animals carried from ancient towns. Within my house guarding me: a pot made from shards unearthed in Jerusalem holds Bible stories; a carpet with 10,000 thread-thin knots tells Chinese Silk Road tales; emus follow points of paint from Aboriginal water hole to water hole; remnants of Rajasthani women's embroidered saris are cut and pieced into a cloth that glitters with desert sun; batik court scenes depict Bali's old capital Klungkung; 100 gold-painted Tibetan Buddhas chant prayers; three masks, ever vigilant, from New Guinea guard me; Indonesian shadow puppets flutter with ideas; beading from a Zimbabwe tribe reveals secrets to Princess Sophie, a papier-mâché parrot from Puerto Vallarta. All tell me stories and I whisper mine while my sandalwood clock keeps its special time. Inside, instead of clockworks, lies a miniature Taj Mahal; inside the Taj Mahal a crypt; inside the crypt, eyelash-thin, lies Mumtaz, the beloved wife of Shah Jehan. Mumtaz, Buddhas, Chinese warriors, New Guinea masks, Princess Sophie, emus—all protect me and give me the time, permission, and beauty I need to create. They are my Mah-Jongg tiles.

# A Jewish Romanian in Oxford

## Maria Roth

### Day 1

For so long I wished to see Oxford, the home of science and beauty.

In just a few hours I have traveled a great distance from my home in Cluj, Romania. I flew from Cluj to Budapest and then to London, and from there took the bus to Oxford.

As I arrive at the bus station in Oxford, I find the city colorful and animated. The crowded streets and bars and throngs of young people are more familiar to me than the high English buses and left-side traffic. The campus is gorgeous. Winning a month-long scholarship to the university looks even better. Oxford looks wonderful and I am eager to discover it. I hope the people are as nice as the taxi driver was.

### Day 2

On my arrival at the college, a porter hands me a bunch of keys and gives me directions to my room. He indicates that I am to follow a long corridor to the other side of the college yard, take the path alongside another building, then through a second yard, and then proceed through a wooden gate. He calls the dormitory the "stables." He does not accompany me to my room; at home we would be nicer to our guests. But I am still eager to see my room.

My room is on the ground floor of this large building, which is surrounded by a beautiful garden. It is July, and the roses and magnolias are in full flower. The building looks nice from outside, but on entering the room, I understand what "stables" means. It must have been only recently transformed to accommodate human guests. There are spider webs. The room is large and smelly, with flea-market furniture that is more or less comfortable but broken here and there. A pipe in the bathroom is leaking, and the wall is all wet, the odor of mold strong. Would this room have ever been assigned to a professor from Western Europe?

I try to get used to the place, however, and I am eager to see the rest of the college. I try to understand all the instructions: about signing up for meals in the senior common room of the college, about mealtimes, emergency procedures, the TV room, the porter's telephone numbers, the college library.

I get up the courage to see the bursar, who is smiling and polite. She takes me on a little tour around the main corridor of the college and then leaves me in the teachers' common room to enjoy an English cup of tea. Later I go back to her to ask about dinner and some towels, which I did not find in the room. She explains that cleaning and repairs are not her responsibilities.

For dinner I am taken to the canteen of the college where about 100 schoolchildren are eating. They are enrolled in summer language classes. The food is acceptable, but the room is noisy. I cannot eat properly. I feel I am going to be sick here, as my son was when he was four and we took him to the seaside, where we ate at a large, cheap restaurant of a second-class hotel.

I go for a short evening walk, which I enjoy, but it starts to rain. I purchase a telephone card and call all three men of mine: my son, my husband, and my father.

They miss me. I hear it in their voices and I feel guilty, not staying home to take care of them. My husband is always unhappy when I go away, yet when I am at home we seldom make any plans to travel together.

I try to rest a little. Perhaps, as my husband said, I should not have left home. I am probably too old for this sort of thing if I care more about my room than about Oxford and accomplishing an old dream.

## Day 3

I go to bed very early, but the strange bed, the smell, and the deep silence make it difficult to relax. It is cold, it is raining, and nobody is around. The large dormitory seems empty. I miss my home and I feel angry. I swear to myself that it is the last time that I apply for an Eastern European scholarship in an elite place.

## Day 4

In the morning, after a bad night, I feel like a complete stranger, surrounded by unfamiliar people, streets, shops, houses, plants, voices, noises, rooms, furniture, bed sheets, smells, and tastes.

For these past three days I have tried to enjoy the sights of Oxford and its history, which I only vaguely understand. Some fifty colleges exist in the central area alone, each one older and more beautiful then the next. Oxford is a place of huge parks, rich museums, stunning cathedrals and churches, and an invaluable cultural heritage in its libraries. But it makes me feel incompetent, left-handed, slow. I try to find information on where I am, what I am looking at and what it means for England's history, for Western culture, for humanity and for myself—something that will be meaningful to me once I get home.

## Day 5

My mind is registering beautiful Oxford, but my senses long for home. Everything is so very different. I try to ease homesickness by finding reminders of home in a bit of food, flowers, birds, squirrels, weather, shops.

When, by chance, I hear people speaking Hungarian or Romanian in the streets, I turn my head around. I spend a pleasant hour chatting with two young Hungarian girls visiting England on their holidays, speaking Hungarian, my maternal language. They are as happy as I am to be able to discuss in our language our impressions of English politeness and how different their ways are of making us feel at home. They tell me how differently they themselves treated their English friends visiting them in Budapest. I tell them how glad I was to receive English guest teachers in my department, and in my home—only a few years ago. My enthusiasm has lessened these past years, so I am not the host I used to be. I am talking to these girls—complete strangers—because I miss my family, my room, and my cat, and my feeling of competence while shopping, working, or talking with friends. I miss the strong coffee, the fresh bread, and the lemon in the otherwise fine English tea, the yogurt without fruits, cheese that's not Cheddar, and the taste of home-grown vegetables. I do enjoy new tastes of salmon, beef stacks, toast and salted butter, chocolate tarts, and olive sauce. But mostly I seek out fried potatoes and chicken, which I prepare at home. From time to time I think about egg salad.

## Day 7

In the evening, alone in the room in this large house in the back of the yard, I struggle with solitude. I do not know the few teachers who come around for the common lunch, and nobody wishes to know me. The loneliness makes me feel, more than ever, no matter how beautiful a place is, that my home is a city in the middle of Transylvania, a city now called Cluj, and once called Kolozsvar, and, at another time, Klausenburg.

Why? What kind of hometown is Cluj? What makes me feel so connected there, even when things go wrong? How can I explain it? Is it in the language I speak, or in my relations with people? Is it in the comfort of home or the security of my job, or is it inside me? I need this space between Oxford and Kolozsvar, to think.

My homesickness does not originate in patriotism. I am critical of Romania and Romanians, which is not surprising for a Jew living in Romania. I do not think Jews are the holiest or the best or the smartest people, or that Romania is the most beautiful country, or that Romanians are the most tolerant or the friendliest people. Nor do I think that Hungarians are the bravest or the most honest. The search for national character is useless, and even dangerous. It amazes me how strange I feel away from home: from my family, my bedroom, my office, the streets of my hometown.

## Day 10

Today Oxford is not so strange. I already know a few nice shops, including some excellent bookshops; I have visited several libraries and museums. I can spend hours on the streets enjoying myself. The leak in the bathroom was repaired and the carpets were vacuumed. I've gotten used to the spiders.

I am still trying to understand why I feel so attached to my home in spite of my lifelong wish to go away from it and live somewhere else. My mind has actually never really accepted that I am a Romanian. I am used to thinking of myself as a Jew, but as a European citizen who lives in Romania.

For at least twenty-five years I have wanted a home away from Romania. But I always had some reason for not leaving. I had a small child. I disliked Israel because of its nationalism, religiosity, and wars.

I blamed my parents and husband; I blamed my age. I was too young to be alone, then I was too old to start over. I blamed my relatives and friends who left Romania and never offered me the slightest help. Whenever I asked them for information, they told me how difficult it was to build a new life, and they advised me not to do it.

I used to think that, with the slightest bit of help, I would by now be somewhere in the West, teaching and counseling children. So many friends and Jewish schoolmates were abroad living a life without the financial concerns we constantly struggle with in Romania. Why did I stay at home? Fear? Inner structure? Now after *alea jacta est*, I am still wondering what kept me home.

## Day 14

Today, I conclude that I like it too much at home.

I've managed to have an acceptable life and I've had too little imagination to set higher standards for myself. If I had had a worse life at home, I would have left it. But there were always things that kept me. I was afraid to lose what I had. I wanted to keep in touch with my parents and have a father for my son, to be able to offer my son a good education, to let him be with his family. I loved my work with children, and was afraid that I would lose it if I could not speak another language well enough.

I wanted a better life—but at home. I was longing for freedom, as others did under communism. I longed to express myself, to have access to information, to be rid of the communist blah-blah and the fear of the secret police. I did not want to hide what I read, what radio stations I listened to, what I talked about with my friends at work. I wanted to have good food for my child without standing in lines and to choose my clothing, my holidays, my music, my books. I wanted to implement better practice models at work. I had had enough of control, and ideology. I secretly hoped for a western lifestyle—but at home.

# Day 17

Our apartment—our actual home—was assigned to us by the Romanian state in the last year of communism. We paid rent to the authorities. I felt like I was the wealthiest person in the world when I got the keys to the "large" apartment on the first floor of a building of fifteen other flats at one of the margins of the city. After 1990, in the new democracy, we, like all beneficiaries of state-owned flats, were given the option of becoming, for a reasonable price, owners.

Before 1989 our apartment's greatest advantage was its access to Hungarian TV. We could thwart the government's vigilant jamming of signals from abroad. We now had access to real information instead of the propaganda we had been receiving three hours a day on Romanian TV, with its permanent actor, Ceausescu. In the evenings we would have friends over to watch Hungarian TV. It brought the dissident movement into our living room, as well as sports, culture and social life in the world.

Our apartment is twice as large as our two previous flats, which had no living rooms. They consisted of only two bedrooms and a very small kitchen, and both were on the ground floor, which made them colder when heating was such a problem in Romania. We were freezing during Fall and Winter. We had acceptable heat only on special occasions: National Celebration Day, Ceausescu's birthday, New Year's Eve, and during a few other communist celebration days. We used small heaters to supplement the building's central heating. Three years ago our apartment caught fire. It was probably caused by the cat, who may have jumped on one of the buttons of the heater. It was a shock for the three of us to see and smell our flat as it filled with smoke. Many of our books were burned.

Lately, we have more stuff than we have space, and from time to time we give things away. Every weekend we give things to two beggar families who come to our door for help, and this feels good. I rarely refuse to give something to beggars. And there are lots of them. This may have something to do with the Jewish religious obligation not to refuse a beggar. In Oxford I have also seen many beggars, but I cannot afford to give them money; I do not feel the same moral obligations away from home.

## Day 19

Actually my home has all the comfort I need. Its most important pieces of furniture are the couch and the TV, which make my evenings comfortable, and my books and laptop, which allow me to work. I also have a washing machine, an espresso coffee-machine, and a microwave.

Washing and dish washing were always my pleasures. My mother could not leave unwashed dishes for later, and I can't either. I have to wash dishes the moment someone has eaten. My son was ten years old and I was still washing everything by hand. When he was smaller, I had a diaper washer; it was small but it was a great help to me. The fifteen-year-old washing machine still works. With cleaning I am less tidy; many things are left to the cleaning woman, who can do it much better.

The pictures on our walls are not valuable, but I love the two watercolor landscapes and the black-and-white engraving of the bukk (beech) woods where I went for walks on Sundays in my childhood and in my son's childhood. Through the years we have always had some posters or copies of paintings on the walls of our apartment.

## Day 21

However small it is, my home has to be clean. Even at the beginning of my professional career, I had to have a cleaning woman, like my mother and my grandmother had, to wash windows and floors, beat carpets and do the ironing. To have a cleaning woman coming once a week was a kind of guarantee of our belonging to the middle class.

My home has to be warm, and my objects in the home must be in a tidy disorder that has my fingerprint on it. I need my familiar objects: old poetry books and novels I read as a schoolgirl as well as some albums, which must be close by although I never touch them. I still have some of the vases that I received from my two grandmothers and parents. Grandma had pictures all over the walls in her large villa, but only one picture is still the property of my family.

Soon after we moved into our apartment, it became small. I never struggled to decorate it; I knew that we could not afford it but I wanted to make it as comfortable as possible. And in contrast to most of the women I know, I never bought myself any jewelery. I have no precious china, silver, or jewels. We have no glass cabinet with lovely knick-knacks like my grandma had. Over the years, the few valuables my mother inherited from her parents were sold in order to buy flats and furniture for my parents, my grandparents, and for us. The last precious pieces went to a person we thought would help my husband get a job. The wonderful hand-painted dishes also contributed to the purchase of some much needed household items. Some smaller silver plates went to doctors. My small heart-shaped gold locket, which I received when I was ten years old, was stolen from me by a telephone installer. As for real wealth, we have nothing at all. But there are tons of books and papers that my husband and I have worked with throughout the twenty-eight years of our professional lives. A lot of work has gone into those books and papers. Most of them belong to the scientific literature of the social sciences. But after all these years, a number of them have lost their relevance outside Romania, and even within Romania, our home.

What, in my home, is Jewish? Not too much. I have a very small menorah, a beautiful Jewish plate, some books explaining Jewish history and religion, and always some matzos in the pantry. The rest is in my mind.

# Day 24

Yesterday a little English girl, about five or six years old, was waiting for her mother who was singing in a choir. After growing tired of drawing, she wrote sentences on a piece of paper: *My mother is the best mother in the wole wrld! I lve you moter so very much.* I wrote the same words, made the same mistakes, forty-five years ago, as did my son eighteen years ago. Only the languages are different. The meaning is universal. It reminded me of how strong my own family ties have been my whole life. As a child, I was very attached to my parents. My mother was my favorite. She was a pediatrician, who visited newborns and children each day and saw another thirty to forty patients in her office. She told me stories about the problems of children and their families, and she let me accompany her on some of her visits. I did not become a physician; I am a psychologist who teaches social workers how to work with families.

As I grew older I understood more about my father's reasons for fearing the country's political situation. He and I had long dinner conversations. But I found my mother's stories the most interesting. She was struggling daily to overcome the socialist health system and to make sure that children had the necessary medication and that their mothers could stay home when their babies were sick.

My parents could not leave their parents, and I could not leave my parents—ever. But my mother left me. Sadly, she died five years ago and I miss her very much. What she and my father gave me was more than love. Together they built a foundation of values for me. They offered me love and independence, they taught me to think with my own head, to trust my own judgment and to question orders. They taught me to believe in rationality, rather than in God's will or the will of others. Most of all, they taught me to appreciate other people regardless of ethnicity, language, or skin color. And they loved the arts. They taught each other and themselves about classical music, painting, sculpting, architecture, and all the basic heritage of humanity. They could read and speak German, French, and English;

they studied these languages in private classes before and during the world war when they were expelled from public schools because they were Jews. I do not know everything they knew, but I am as open as they were to learning about other people's cultures.

## Day 27

Is my city one where women like me feel at home? Who are "women like me"? I am a Hungarian-speaking Jewish woman educated in a Romanian school, who then became a psychologist and is now teaching social work. There are not too many people with backgrounds like mine. A woman of fifty whose parents were both Jewish and who is still living in Romania is like the last Mohican.

All Jews of my generation left Romania a long time ago.

## Day 28

When I visited the States I was amazed that people go everywhere by car. I do not drive and prefer to walk for hours in the streets, mostly in the central areas of the city. My city, Kolozsvar, is not a dangerous city; nobody is afraid to walk in the streets. And yet, I still go home before night falls because I am afraid of the dark. Since my fiftieth birthday, I feel that I am slowing down, my senses are not so sharp, and I think more about safety—in the streets, in my home, on the bus. Things like holes in the asphalt, inattentive bus drivers, dark streets in cold winter nights, nervous car drivers, loud-speaking people, unlocked doors at the entrance of my building make me nervous. But these fears pale in comparison with those I experience alone in a flat in Oxford, a city in which I know no one.

When I think about home, I think about identity. My parents told me we were Jewish, though they were not religious at all. Their deepest beliefs were that people must think for themselves and not "believe" what is preached. But I was born in 1954, and the pain of the Holocaust was still acute. Our relatives had died in Auschwitz. My father's father took me to the synagogue and blessed me each day during the summers I stayed with them. I could never relate to any identity other than the Jewish one. My husband is a Hungarian Christian, but I kept my Jewish family name. I did not want anyone to accuse me of hiding behind another national identity. My parents accepted my husband without comment—at least to me. They were upholding their principle that ethnicity does not interfere with a person's character.

## Day 29

I am going back home in two days. I am not anxious anymore. Oxford is beautiful and I feel independent. It took coming to Oxford to realize this. In a few days I will assume the responsibilities of home again. I have shouldered responsibilities since my son was born. I was twenty-four then, working in a school for mentally handicapped children in Vasarhely. Most of the children in my class were gypsies. I enjoyed those children as much as any other children I have worked with. As for my son, I felt attached to him from the moment he was born and tried hard to be a good mother. I was young and had far too many ambitions for him, but we are close and like to spend time together. I have always been the protective Jewish *mamele* who wants to control everything, to know that her son is safe. My profession, however, taught me that overprotection is wrong, and I forced myself to let him fall freely. But my nature was against me. He ended up learning my anxiety. Probably this tendency is second nature to Jews since the Holocaust, or even before it. Unlike us, I suppose that some people have succeeded in overcoming it.

    The thought of being surrounded by family and familiar objects and duties—is relaxing. I may even try to participate in the Jewish community. When I see all the elderly people who work to supplement their small pensions, I feel more pity then pride. Many are left alone by the deaths of their loved ones. Some lost family members in the deportations, which they themselves survived. I still struggle as to how best talk to them. By the time I am wise enough, none of them will be alive.

# In the Margin

## Madeline Tiger

Why do I, who always deny category,
a proud Jew who never holds on
under defined faith, why
do I want my words to stretch
your guidelines,
and push the walls of your book

to erect a little chapter
right here in the margin?
and whisper *midrash*
in the Maccabbean evening? Why
if I say *No Sabbath prayer here*
(even though I love hearing Elijah my grandson singing
in his house at their *Shabbat*) and if I insist
*No eight days of marking guerrilla victory miracle here*
(even though the Langs live in my blood
and Viennese villages survived long enough
to allow us life, and Granny could speak of her
*zeliga* mother, and I love *polichinta*) . . . Why
if I don't teach prayers or buy Kosher or pronounce
*Chanukah* at the back of my throat,
do I want you to note what is here,
to note: a home as a place one comes back to

every day
for the peace and the smell a child might describe
because that's what a good house holds.

I want you to note that my early orphaned mother
is there, with her parents, on my bedroom wall;
and my unfathered father is there, with his sisters
staring through their serious Ashkenazi eyes
on my dining room wall, where they meet each other
and celebrants eat roast chicken, Granny's recipe,
and the garlic is back

May I insist—how to insist?—
that a little house on the margin of days
with no *Sabbath* and no *Seder*
and even Thanksgiving taken away
is never empty. The plants grow,
the light shines, the music beats,
the kitchen fills with dark smells,
acorn squash in cinnamon
and a new pot of hazelnut decaf
to keep me going every night.

Some Jews live beyond any rules.
New lines may be
inscribed
in the Book of Life,
and my little house—empty
except for my music,
my greenery, my clear air,
my pillows and shoes—
is perfectly fit
for a Jewish woman
growing old
with her own rituals.

# To the Smell of Sea and Pickle

## Dalia Kaveh

*Translated from the Hebrew by Linda Stern Zisquit*

This is the courtyard
full of tins and cats.
This is the not-so-high fence
that encloses it.
This is the street,
this is the corner with
always new puddles,
and this is the roof that opens double,
and this is the window through which a distance
opens to the waiting fields.
This is the dusky woods,
mimosa trees projecting yellow.
On branches of dryness
snails develop,
and winter's beauty in them—
longings, longings.
This is the shame,
this is the silence,
the beginning of desire.
This is the youthful guard,
my secret love.

This is the neighborhood madwoman
who covers her money with rags,
and Haim the friendly shoemaker.
This is the floor,
the mother and her two daughters tired
in view of the Araucaria,
on its trunk the cats
have lost their claws.
This is the introspective man
lighting up a pipe,
in back of a desk—
stamps and sweets.

And this is the too hot summer
that sends people to their balconies,
to the smell of sea and pickles.
This is friendship,
street songs,
choruses of hopscotch and jump rope.
Behind bushes in the garden a hiding place.
This is pain like
the stalk of the mercury weed
bearing serrated leaves,
male and female separately.
This is the lovely,
this is the awful,
this is the generous.
This is the feeble,
this the distinct
and the miraculous
within an empty space of
dandelions and nettles.

# Isibaya (The Home)

## CHA JOHNSTON

*In African tradition respect is paid to the home or space where significant events happen, where offerings are made or where answers are found through accessing the ancestors and respecting traditions.*

    I have homed
    in these sacred spaces
    crawling with snake heads
    African, Jewish, White, Naked
    Homeless
    like old statues
    tanned by ink and lore
    or new paper that has eaten trees
    seen life and death many times
    in a scripture or symbol
    or pouring of texture upon a page
    by a boy on a cross dreaming himself an artist.

    The old way is to die on a river bank
    feeding the wolverines
    feeding the hunger of the moon's decant.

    The old way is to harvest midnight's aura
    trance in her attire
    through biddings and forbiddings

flicking ash to the fire of secrets
where temple calls not to Jesuit bread
or Dingaan's ox
but to the finer sprigs of the spirit
bartered in the unknown unclothed underside
of God's youth and age
Goddess's great hind legs pushing
agnostics to their cause.

Homed in the tongue of man
I have cried for release from religion
or lack of it
praying for snake to forgive me
for mather to tusk me back to the beginning.

She who left me with the apple
in the compress of hunger
fingering love in food
Persephone's Adamless vial.

To Isibaya, who lives on the open plains,
this is good
this is grain and gold leaf and bowl's dancing.
To Baba Yaga who drags stragglers to their death
to find their way
this is poison and berry leaf and skirts lancing.

It is the way of food without the mother
or the way of home without the mother
or the way of heart without the mother
or the way of spirit without the mother.

It is the Isibaya song
the finding one's way home.

It is the mating call and skin offerings
the grand cross at its cairn
with great and little rivers knowing your name.

It is the length of time it takes
to know everything and nothing in the walk
to hear mama calling
from within
to hear the lion's singing
becoming the strange landscape of home
seeing through home
letting home go
thanking snake for his kindness.

# III

# Language and Creativity

❖

# Yiddishland

## Ellen Cassedy

A soft rain was falling as a white-haired woman slowly made her way to the microphone in the courtyard of Vilnius University. "*Tayere talmidim!*" she began. "Dear students!" I leaned forward to catch her words through the pattering of drops on my umbrella. The old woman was a member of the tiny, aging Jewish community in the capital of Lithuania. Her name was Blume. "How fortunate I am," she said in a quavering voice, "that I have lived long enough to see people coming to Vilnius to study Yiddish."

Seventy-five of us huddled together on wooden benches under the heavy Baltic sky. We had come from all over the globe to spend a month at the Vilnius Yiddish Institute. Some were college students looking for credits; others, middle-aged like me, had arrived in the former Jerusalem of the North in search of something else.

Years earlier, when my mother died, I'd developed a yearning for the language of my ancestors—the Jewish ones, that is (my gentile father's family hails from Germany and Great Britain). My mother had used the old Jewish vernacular only sparingly, like a spice, but when she died I found myself missing the hints of the old world that I used to hear in her pungent Yiddish expressions. At the window on a rainy day: "A *pliukhe!*" ("A downpour!") In the kitchen: "Hand me that *shisl.*" ("Hand me that bowl.") On the telephone: "The woman's a *makhsheyfe.*" ("The woman's a witch.")

When my mother was alive, I could count on her to keep hold of the past. Now that she was dead, not only had I lost her, but all those who'd gone before seemed to be slipping out of reach, too. I hadn't been able to save my mother from cancer, but maybe by joining the Yiddish revival I could help to save *mame-loshn*, the old mother tongue. Maybe Yiddish, which has been called "the linguistic homeland of a people without a home," could offer me the comforting sense of continuity that had been ruptured by my mother's death. In helping to keep that cultural homeland alive, perhaps I could find a way home myself.

I started with an elementary Yiddish phrase book, then tried an evening class at the Jewish college near my home in Philadelphia. The Germanic sounds felt comfortable in my ears and mouth, and the Hebrew alphabet was daunting but not impossible. I listened to tapes, copied out grammar exercises, and thumbed my dictionary till the binding broke. Bit by bit, I began to feel a connection to the language once common in lanes, meeting halls, and market squares on both sides of the Atlantic Ocean.

Now in Vilnius, or Vilna, the former capital of the Yiddish world, I hoped to deepen that connection. Lithuania, in my childhood, had always seemed utterly inaccessible, as if it existed in another dimension, like Atlantis or Narnia. No one from my family who'd made it across the Atlantic from there had ever been back. Yet here I was, looking up into the same sky that had sheltered my great-grandmother Asne and her dairy farm and my great-grandfather Dovid and his study house. Under this sky, my grandfather Yankl had been a *yeshive bokher* (student) and then a socialist before running to America to escape the draft. Here, during the Nazi era, my Uncle Velvl had been confined behind barbed wire in the Shavl ghetto. And here, after returning from Dachau, my Uncle Aron had been arrested and exiled to Siberia. As the rain continued to fall and the damp courtyard darkened, I shivered. It was a hard place, this land of my forebears—a country where Jews and their culture had been systematically exterminated—a curious place to come looking for a sense of belonging.

The next morning I hurried through the courtyard and up a steep stairway into a classroom that was crammed with four rows of battered wooden desks. The Yiddish instructor, a bearded scholar, did not actually carry a stick, like a *melamed*—a teacher in the one-room Jewish schoolhouse of old—but his rules were strict. Before every class, we were to study the assigned text with care. Questions would be allowed only about words that did not appear in our dictionaries—and having written one of the dictionaries himself, he knew exactly what was in them. Not a word of English was permitted.

As we took turns reading aloud, I kept a finger glued to the page. If my concentration faltered for a second, I was lost. When the teacher spoke, whole paragraphs went by in a blur. For some reason, my hand kept flying into the air with questions and comments. The moment I opened my mouth, however, I realized I had no idea how to get to the end of a sentence. In this language that was not really my own, it was as if I were two people. One was an impractical idealist who set off with supreme confidence into the unknown, while the other was a benighted worker who ran ahead, frantically trying to build a road for the journey.

Outside the classroom, amid the pastel facades and crisp spires of twenty-first-century Vilnius, traces of the old Jewish world were few and far between. But the last Yiddish speakers of Vilnius led us on long walks that began on cobblestoned Zydu *gatve* (Jewish Street). Blume returned with Fania and Rokhl—stumpy, tireless women with strong, short legs. Standing in the scuffed grass of a vacant lot, they described the centuries-old Great Synagogue that had once towered over the surrounding study houses, the famous Strashun Library, the schools and theaters that had crowded the narrow lanes when they were young. Back then, they said, the streets resounded with Yiddish, as learned rabbis brushed up against fish peddlers, and young people like my grandfather engaged in fierce debates over politics and religion. Then came the Nazi invasion and the ghetto. Some 70,000 Jews were jammed into the old Jewish quarter on this very spot where we were standing amid trash bins and dusty playground swings.

"One night," Rokhl said, "I was awakened by the barking of dogs. Outside my window, the police were driving long columns of Jews. The people had their children by the hand and their belongings tied up in bed sheets, white sheets in the black night."

More than 90 percent of Lithuania's 240,000 Jews died during World War II. Some of our elderly guides on this tour had fled to safety before the massacre began; others, like Rokhl, had escaped from the ghetto and joined the Red Army in the forests. Now, sometimes weeping, sometimes radiant, they talked and talked—about the world that used to be, about the people who were no more, about their own miraculous survival.

The flat where I lived with my roommate, Shirley, a retired kindergarten teacher from California, was located in the middle of the former ghetto. In the evenings, we used an old-fashioned key to open the creaking wooden door into our courtyard and then climbed the stairs to our rooms. Bent over our books at the kitchen table, we did massive amounts of homework, whispering under our breath as we riffled our dictionaries. Oy, those verbs, with the *umge*-this and the *oysge*-that, the *aroysge*-this and the *farge*-that! Every paragraph was an ordeal. On top of each sentence I penciled a spidery layer of interpretation, dividing the verbs and the compound nouns into their component parts, underlining words I didn't know, double-lining those that should be stressed when reading aloud, enclosing phrases in parentheses, numbering and rearranging the elements of especially convoluted expressions. As I grew tired, the letters swam before my eyes until the page of sinuous Hebrew characters resembled a sheet of matzo. At times I was near tears. Why couldn't I understand? Why wouldn't this language—this comfortable old mother tongue—reach out to embrace me?

In the mornings, I began to awaken with Yiddish words on my tongue, which I would savor with a slice of dense black bread topped with butter and cheese from Rokiskis—the very town where my great-grandmother had operated her dairy—and little knobby cucumbers. One week the market offered tiny apricots, and the next, small purple plums. Here in the old world, there was no abundance. Only the *shabes tish*—our weekly Friday night celebration at the Jewish community center—was lavish. The long tables spread with snowy cloths were loaded with candles and wine and platters of fruit and nuts, cheese and kasha and challah that tasted just right. Late into the night, we sang endless *nigunim*, old wordless melodies full of joy and sorrow.

Day after day, our teachers guided us into the most intimate linguistic nooks and crannies. One morning we pondered the mysteries of verb "aspects": the differences among "I kiss," "I am kissing," and "I keep on kissing." Another time we ran our tongues over long strings of adjectives formed from nouns: oaken door, woolen glove, golden ring, clay pot. On yet another day we learned that *krenken* is to get sick, but *krenklen*, with an added "l," is to fall ill again and again in a less life-threatening way. Later on, we were tickled by the playful variety of Yiddish diminutives: Blume, Blumele, Blumke, Blumkele. More and more, I found words emerging suddenly from the mist, shining and clear, or whole sentences popping out of my mouth fully formed. At the end of every session, we sat back and listened as the instructor read from his favorite texts in a sonorous and elegiac voice. A *mekhaye*—a great pleasure.

In the evenings, as I worked my way through my assignments, vivid scenes began to come into view:

One story I read ushered me into a snug wooden house on a chilly *shabes* afternoon. The cottage was sunk in deep snow—just as, for me, the meaning of the text was buried under the blanket of a difficult alphabet. Inside, a beginning reader named Yidl opened a holy book. As Yidl used a thick index finger to sound out the words, the two of us made our way down the page together.

Another story in my textbook took place at the turn of the twentieth century in the courtyard of the Great Synagogue—the very courtyard where Blume, Fania, and Rokhl had told their tales. On the first page, thousands upon thousands of Jews were gathered for the funeral of a famous Talmudist. Slowly, in an upper story high above the crowd, a window began to open, and as a curious little boy leaned out to survey the scene, I leaned out with him.

A third text brought me to a dark corner of the Vilna ghetto during World War II, where a writer sat scribbling, imagining himself to be a bell whose somber tones shattered the silence of the black ghetto night. How privileged I felt to be able to catch the tolling of that bell.

Halfway through the month, along with these literary characters, I began to sense another set of characters beside me as well: my mother with her love of a tasty turn of phrase; my grandfather with his old-age devotion to Carl Sandburg and Mark Twain and other giants of American literature; my great-grandfather Dovid, whose beard had quivered over the Talmud; and finally, perhaps not a reader at all, my great-grandmother Asne, the dairywoman and mother of nine, who must have been possessed of a fearsome persistence. Even more than I'd hoped, learning Yiddish had linked me to my ancestors and brought the past to life.

On weekends, I visited the grim headquarters of the Soviet secret police, now a museum, where Uncle Aron was imprisoned before being sent to the gulag, and the tumble-down alleys of the old Shavl ghetto where Uncle Velvl had been confined. I traveled to the tiny hamlet where my grandfather grew up—not even a crossroads, really, just a stand of trees and a scattering of houses and barns and marigolds nodding in the sun. In the town of Rokiskis, I walked down Synagogo *gatve*, where three wooden study houses used to stand—the green one, the red one, and my great-grandfather's yellow one. On the outskirts of town, I stood in the green glade where the Jews of Rokiskis had been lined up and shot. As the wind stirred the leaves of the birch trees overhead, I listened, and in my head I answered. *Ikh bin do*, I whispered, *I am here*.

Back in Vilnius, at the urging of my Rokiskis guide, I paid a call on Ida, an eighty-three-year-old woman with strong features and penetrating eyes, who had grown up not far from the three colorful study houses. "*Kumt arayn*" ("Come in"), she said as she ushered me into her parlor, where a table was set with cream cakes dotted with red currants and sour cherries in a silver bowl. A visit from a Rokiskis *landsman*—a fellow countryman or descendant like me—was clearly a special occasion.

Ida was one of only two in her entire family to have survived the war, she told me in Yiddish as we sipped tea from delicate china cups. Every September, she said, she travels to the mass murder site in the forest near Rokiskis, the same place I had just been, to honor the memory of her loved ones.

There was something she wanted from me, something I couldn't figure out. Again she explained, and again I strained to understand. After a while her meaning became clear. She wanted to know if she had been visiting the right place all these years. Were the bones of her mother and father, her brothers and her aunts and uncles and cousins and grandparents, truly buried beneath the grassy tufts of this particular clearing? Or were they in fact lying in another killing field, in Obeliai, a few miles up the road? Was there a list somewhere?

I shook my head. *Neyn*, I said, I didn't believe there was such a list. And no, I couldn't answer her question. But what I could do, as her attempt to tend to the dead touched my heart, was hold her hand. I could hear her words, and I could respond, however haltingly, in soft syllables of *mame-loshn*, our mother tongue.

As our month drew to a close, my roommate Shirley began to relax over her books at the kitchen table. She dreamed of her swing under the orange tree back in Los Angeles. I kept going full-steam, still wrestling with every line of every assigned text, still looking up every unfamiliar word in the dictionary, then walking for hours through the city, taking in the pink walls that glimmered in the last light, the squares where young people—the inheritors of this land with its huge and complicated history—sat in the outdoor cafés under the stars.

On the last day of class, we finished a story written after the Holocaust in which the narrator finds himself pulling a wagon piled high with dead bodies. *So it is for all of us*, I thought, *as we go forward lugging our past behind us.* It was our hardest story yet, a thicket of obscure words and fiendishly complex constructions, but I didn't mind. I'd come to feel that in Yiddishland, this place of love and of pain, it was the effort itself that mattered. Simply trying—to listen, to understand, to speak—brought a deep satisfaction and the sense of connection I'd been seeking.

At the graduation ceremony, the sun shone in a blue sky, and there were flowers and herring and vodka. Alas, Blume was too ill to attend, but Fania and Rokhl were there to send us on our way. We gave a kiss, we kissed, we kept on kissing, and crying. It was hard to leave.

# Silence

## Dalia Kaveh

*Translated from the Hebrew by Linda Stern Zisquit*

And immediately after they left
the house streamed toward me
and the silence was projected.
And immediately after they went
the red burst out of the petunias,
burst out and was melted to the ceiling
and the room was lit.
Then trembling purple passed
through the heart of the oil paintings
and burned in them
and turned from them
to the book jackets,
grasped a lamp
and stormed the windowpane and hastened
to the isolated clay pots
awakening bonfires in them
but escaping from their heat
to the cold glass sea
poured like dark tea
and the room was wrapped in fog.

# The Girl in the Balcony

## Angelina Muñiz-Huberman

The scene takes place on a balcony. As if it were a scene from a classical play. A mother is talking to her daughter. It is a cool afternoon in the Condesa borough of Mexico City. The year is 1942, in the middle of the Second World War. The child is listening carefully; she is only six years old but she can tell that something important is about to be said. The girl is leaning lightly on the balcony and the mother has traces of a smile on her face.

Why choose a balcony to tell something that might be crucial for the child's future? Maybe because it is a remote part of the house? A part that seems separated, that seems to float in the air? An intimate space? A space where a secret can be kept?

Thus, in a spaceless space and in timeless time, compelled by the concentration of instant words, truth is revealed to the small child. The light of knowledge illuminates the balcony and now she knows that she is one of the children of Israel. Her mother tells her how for centuries her ancestors would transmit the secret of their origins, always from mother to daughter, in a veiled manner and in a secluded place, so as to avoid persecution. And now, the child has been handed the responsibility of continuing with this tradition. She has promised never to forget it and to transmit it, in due time, to her own children.

Light illuminates the balcony, but a seal of secrecy has been imposed. Knowing that every minute counts, the mother continues her confession. She teaches her daughter to make a sign in order to be recognized by other fellow Jews: with hands extended, the fingers are united in pairs to imitate the form of the first letter of *Shaddai*, the divine name.

With each day that passes, a new stone is added to the mosaic, a new piece of the puzzle finds its place. Little by little, the girl recognizes the complex pattern of her family. As far as memory can go, the family had lived for centuries in Spain. In 1492, when the Expulsion Edict against Sephardic Jews was issued, her family did not go into exile, but rather stayed and was forced to convert into Christianity, increasing thus the ranks of Crypto-Jews, also called Marranos.

If her family did not leave Spain in 1492, what is she doing in Mexico in 1942? It is now her turn to experience exile. Her parents, Spanish Republicans, went into exile during the Civil War. The girl was born in France, and then, a few months before the Second World War was declared, they were just in time to take a boat to any place in the American Continent. The boat was bound for Cuba, where they stayed for three years and then went to Mexico.

Once living in Mexico, the family moved several times. There was a trip to New York, in 1945, to reunite with part of the family that had fled from the Nazi persecution.

Back again in Mexico and at school, the girl meets children who are survivors of concentration camps. She listens carefully to their stories, because one day she will be a writer and she will consider it her duty to tell such stories.

This way, a world of exile surrounds the child: the Jewish and the Spanish Republican exiles. From then on, she would think of herself as a stranger. Once, when playing in the street, a drunkard shouted at her: *güereja judía*, which means, "coward blond Jewess." At other times she was called a *gachupina* (which is a disrespectful way of referring to Spaniards) and all the sins of the conquistadores were attributed to her.

She got used to accumulating exiles and to taking refuge in an inner world where imagination and freedom reigned supreme. Without knowing it, she was laying down the basis of her future as a writer.

Years later, she combined the story of her own exiles in the figure of Santa Teresa in *Morada interior*, the first New Historical novel of contemporary Mexican literature. *Tierra adentro and La guerra del Unicornio* deal with the lives of Sephardic Jews in Medieval and Renaissance times. In *La lengua florida* she compiled an anthology of Sephardic literature. *Las raíces y las ramas* was dedicated to explaining the Kabbalah and its manifestations. For another book she chose the title of *El mercader de Tudela* to narrate the life of a famous medieval traveler, Benjamin of Tudela. Or the exile of the Spanish republicans that appears in *Dulcinea encantada, Las confidentes*, as well as in her poems and short stories. And again, a combination of both is present in *Areúsa en los conciertos* and *El siglo del desencanto*.

However, it will be in her pseudomemoirs—a genre of her own creation—where she develops the idea of a house being the key place that determines the meaning of life, knowledge, desire, and creativity. Each one of these books begins with the description of the inhabited space and from it a particular point of view emerges that sets the tone for the pages that follow.

Thus, "home" is not just the actual living space but also one's own interior space where everything is possible and where life cannot be thwarted. It is no coincidence that the first novel written by the girl in the balcony was called *Interior Abode (Morada interior)*.

And it is so that the girl on the balcony—who is no other than myself—invents her life within four walls, a window, a chair, and a solid oak table. Could there be a better home?

# The Music and Language of Home

## Sara Schwarzbaum

Jews have rarely found a place to call home for extended periods and my family migrated from continent to continent for a very long time. In 1939, my thirteen-year-old mother traveled from Poland to Russia with her widowed father, a man who, in more recent times, would have been called a "hippie." That same year my father fled from Poland to Russia, leaving behind his parents and sisters, never to see them again. My parents met one another in Russia, having escaped the fate that didn't spare their families. They married in 1945 when the war ended, and returned to Poland to count the relatives they'd lost: my father lost 105; my mother stopped counting. But they also found cousins who had survived and with whom they settled in West Germany. My sister was born in Munich in 1948. After seven years my parents were eager to leave Germany. Who could blame them? If you were Jewish, you, too, would have chosen Argentina over Germany, even though some remorseless Nazis ended up in Argentina, as well.

My parents, grandparents, and several cousins settled in Buenos Aires, which was then a cosmopolitan city whose inhabitants spoke Spanish, wore Italian styles, studied French in high school, and frequented cafés that reminded them of Europe. When I was born in Buenos Aires in 1953, my father was barely making a living, Evita was still alive, and Jorge Luis Borges was finishing another one of his masterpieces.

My parents brought to their home in Argentina the languages, cultures, and the music of all the countries they had lived in: the Jewish Poland of their childhood, the Communist Russia of their youth, and the postwar Germany of their first years as a married couple. They also brought with them a number of relatives. In the apartment in Buenos Aires where I spent the first year of my life lived my parents, my sister, my Russian-speaking grandmother, who had married my widowed grandfather, and several unmarried cousins. My grandparents slept in the bedroom, my parents, my sister, and I in the living room, and my father's cousins slept in the kitchen, where they were constantly engaged in loud political discussions in Yiddish, and played chess till 3 a.m.

During that first year of my life, my sister, who was four years old, spoke German to my parents and to me, my mother and father spoke Polish to each other but not to us, my grandfather spoke Yiddish to my sister and to my mother, but not to his wife who understood only Russian. The neighbor across the hall spoke Spanish but nobody understood him. And when my parents didn't want the neighbors to understand any of us, they too spoke in Yiddish. My grandfather, who lived in Buenos Aires for the rest of his long life, never learned a word of Spanish; my father spoke it with a heavy accent; my mother, the one with the musical ear, learned it effortlessly. It wasn't until I went to first grade in the public school around the corner from where I lived that I was exposed to Spanish. In high school I became proficient in French. So, when somebody wants to know which is my maternal language, I don't know how to answer. For me, all of them are.

My parents also brought their music to Argentina; it was another language in my childhood home, a presence as real as the relatives who lived with us or came to visit. During my early years in Buenos Aires, my grandparents listened to records of German lieder sung by Polish tenors and Hungarian sopranos; and my mother wept while listening to Russian folk songs. My father developed a fondness for Spanish flamenco, Mexican boleros, and Argentinean tango. In the shower, though, he always whistled Puccini, Verdi, or Mozart operas, a taste for which he had developed early in his life. My father loved classical music and would tell us stories about the great Russian composers while we sat around the kitchen table. I remember the day I learned that Chopin was Polish, not French; that Mendelssohn and the Gershwins were Jewish; and that Beethoven used German folk melodies in his symphonies. How did my father know so much? He hadn't even gone to high school! On Saturday nights the dining room table was moved to the side to make room for dancing relatives who liked to swing with Benny Goodman, Duke Ellington, George and Ira Gershwin, Cole Porter, and Louis Armstrong. On Sunday mornings my sister and I were awakened by orchestras or chamber ensembles playing symphonies, sonatas, and double concertos. At the dinner table and during Jewish holidays my grandfather sang traditional Yiddish songs, and we all joined him. Yiddishkeit emanated from our house and flowed through me along with all the other languages and music.

My mother had learned the Russian folk songs in her Siberian home where she lived during the war. When she was seventeen she used to go dancing on Saturday nights even though she didn't have the right shoes or clothing. She always said these were the best years of her life, and I know that they really were the best because although she was cold and hungry most of the time she was young. My mother loved American standards and jazz; every Friday morning she went to the record store and brought home a new record that she would play over and over until my father learned to whistle it. He learned some songs, like "Cheek to Cheek," right away; others, like "Porgy and Bess," took him a bit longer to learn.

In the mornings I spoke Spanish when I attended public elementary school, and in the afternoons I attended Yiddish school, where I learned more songs in Yiddish and Hebrew. My Argentinean girlfriends wondered why I never spoke about Evita. My mother was too busy feeding all of us, learning Spanish, and helping my dad with his new sweater-manufacturing business to talk about Evita. When I entered high school I realized that I was different from other girls not only because I didn't know much about Evita, but also because I spoke Yiddish and didn't speak French. I told my father that I wanted to study French like the other girls, which I did, though he continued to speak Yiddish to me until he died not long ago.

By the late sixties my grandparents had moved out and the unmarried cousins had found Argentinean wives, though they never stopped their chess games and heated political discussions in our kitchen. I became a typical South American high school student, embracing the Beatles and rock and roll. Tangos, boleros, and sambas were the soundtrack of my life, but I didn't know it until years later, when nostalgia crept into my life. When I finished my degree in clinical psychology in Argentina, I moved to the United States for graduate studies; it had become clear to me that I couldn't make a living as a psychologist if I stayed in Buenos Aires. Architects, doctors, accountants, and lawyers were arriving at similar conclusions and soon many Argentinean professionals left for Spain, Brazil, Mexico, and the United States. When I moved in my early thirties, the only English I knew were the words of the Beatles' songs and it took me years to realize that there was more to living in the United States than learning English. I didn't realize how long it would take me to get established in this country because of the different language and culture. Luckily, I must have inherited my mother's ear for music and language, so it took me less time than it usually takes an immigrant to learn English.

I don't intend to confuse individuals who see me or hear me speak for the first time. People who speak only Polish, Russian, or Spanish may take one look at me and erroneously assume that I could not possibly understand what they are saying. Some people over seventy who still speak Yiddish can hardly believe that I do too. Not infrequently, at the grocery store somebody starts to argue, curse, or reveal something intimate in front of me, unsuspecting.

When I do reveal my language abilities or my family background to anyone, expressions on people's faces reveal that they are perplexed. If I am from South America, why do I have Polish parents, a Russian grandmother, and a German sister? If I speak Spanish, how can I be Jewish? If I am a Latina, why am I fair-skinned? If I came to America as an adult, why do I speak English so well? And—this is my favorite—if what I speak is really Spanish, why does it sound like Italian? Latin Americans sometimes look at me in disbelief: Can a white person speak Spanish like that?

The ongoing blending of my Eastern European, Jewish, Latin American, and American identity surprises many members of my family. It took me years to learn, but I became a soccer mom in spite of my notion that kids should play soccer without adult interference; I joined the PTA before I knew what the letters stood for, and became a room mother in my daughter's second-grade class. I organized Halloween parties without understanding the connection between frightening and fun; I learned about local politics, grassroots movements, the tenure system, and managed care; figured out how to talk politely at board meetings, subduing my natural tendencies for animation and argumentation. If I try really hard, I can have dinner ready by 6 p.m., although when my American husband is out of town I don't eat until 9 p.m., the South American way. I still have trouble controlling the urge to kiss people on the cheek at my book club and faculty meetings, and I definitely do not know what to do with my hands when I remember suddenly that I am not supposed to hug and kiss my adult children's friends when I first meet them.

I may appear to have become an American but there is a less visible part of me that longs for a different lifestyle, different relationships, and definitely more kisses at board meetings. I never felt that I fit in with the other soccer moms, I didn't attend church on Sundays and they weren't interested in the novels of Gabriel Garcia Márquez and Isaac Bashevis Singer. Nor did they rush to see every Holocaust movie that came out.

I am nostalgic for music styles that I don't get to hear often, and I fantasize about starting my own radio station: I'd play Brazilian samba, Argentinean tango, Russian folk songs, American standards, country and bluegrass, German lieder. I don't know anyone else who's home music library contains Caetano Veloso, Susana Rinaldi, Brahms, Mozart, Nora Jones, Louis Armstrong, Dolly Parton, Ofra Haza, and Chava Alberstein.

My mother says I have changed, but I didn't know I would end up like this. I can worry like a Jewish mother, get into arguments like a Russian sailor, cook like an Italian, lie in the sun with zero SPF like a Caribbean, and act like an American feminist. Most of the time I accept the challenges of my multiple identities, but whenever I have had enough of my chameleon-like self, I sit on the couch, listen to a tango or a Yiddish folk song, cry, and wonder: Which is the real me? Each personality trait I show and each music style I love represents a different part of me—the person I was while I was growing up, the person I almost lost when I left Argentina, and the person I became while living in America.

# Here

## Judith Ilson Taylor

Here is the road
(a shadow   a field   a shadow)
that leads from there to
this gate
this garden
this stream
pouring through the dark.

And here? A map
folded in my palm, my pocket
the cuff of my sleeve.
The destination is an equation:
longing times time
plus letting go
divided by equals.
Solve for story:
a table
bread
four pears on a plate
a bowl of salt
and singing

        a skillet   a ladle
        a kettle   a chair
        a shadow   a lamp
        a shadow.

See! The word
on my lips
filling my mouth
like water
the scent of melting wax
sweet wine.

Starlight drapes the bones
of my tent. The curtain glows.
I live in the question.
Not knowing the answer
is home.

# Posit

## Linda Stern Zisquit

Ten measures of beauty came down into the world; nine were taken by Jerusalem, one by the rest of the world.
—Tractate Kiddushin

Ten parts of suffering came down into the world; nine were taken by Jerusalem, one by the rest of the world.
—Avot d'Rabbi Natan

    Had Rachel not looked up
    Jacob would not have seen her.
    There would have been no water,
    no winding dream,

    no tribe or unrelenting
    portion of sadness
    dispersed on his land, his Jerusalem,
    and I would not have promised

    to gather them home. But Rachel
    saw him and he loved her.
    She was barren and she suffered
    and she followed him.

So I have this heaviness
to bear. Her life before him
had also the dailiness of lives,
an hour at which she would rise and go

to the well. Then out of the blue
her future came crashing against her lids
when she looked up, those hours changed,
and I was moved to his, another well.

# Morning Exercise

### Linda Stern Zisquit

Distance doesn't matter. Not dreams of home
or morning filtered through a darker pane
or the timbre of his voice in every room
or blaming every cruelty on the place

or letters no longer expected, unreceived
or pigeons streaming bloodless through the sky.
Only this wafer of unbending light redeemed
a song by all the children passing by:

So this is your home, so new, so new.
And these are its walls, so thin, so fair.
And this is the dance, adieu, adieu.
And these are your eyes, not here, not there.

Distance doesn't speak. Just green leaves
Push their way through a rusty screen.
Jasmine fills the porch as cactus pins
Prick the palm of memory, burning in.

# Renaissance

## Linda Stern Zisquit

Pots scrubbed,
there is no suicide!
Sun draws its pattern,
its silk on everything.
Morning lets go
softly, softly.
I love surfaces,
sky is another floor
or mirror
and everyone glitters
a little. Even the ones crying
in their cars, windows
cranked down, motors purring
in disaffection, even the ones trying
to wear covers, to go backward
into winter and snow.
Tears and oppression
weigh less heavy
as I coax them into the street
with my perfect flesh,
my nature in love with salt,
my hair asking the wind
to part it like feathers

begging to be admired.
Kitchen stacked,
vegetable peeler tucked in its drawer,
berries whole and fresh
and no trace of death.

# Line of Defense

## Linda Stern Zisquit

I don't let the news in at dawn.
I have rules for morning hours,
my ear strained to the warble
and whistle of returning birds.
If only I knew their names
or could decipher, on first
encounter, a plane circling
from a formation veering home,
wings flapping as if the sky's
performance deserved applause.
It's mad here, to maneuver
a day around explosions,
or to hold my pen as if
my words could keep danger
at bay, my son's safety
locked in this little plan.

An artist who paints the desert
mixes rosebuds and ashes
to harness gods that dwell
in hearths, to bring her daughter
health, protect her son.
And in the resin and sand

and pigment spilling around
I feel the force of matter
moving in perfect rhythm
with her love. I want
a poem like her painting,
a sensation of having
something in my control.

# IV
# Family and Tradition

❖

# I, May I Find Home

—after Yehuda Amichai

## Dorothy Field

I, may I find home. I have lived too long
in echoing rooms, darkness
making more darkness, too long between brocade
and squalor, an undeclared war
where bridges are targets and difference
a cudgel, too long amid shredded garments.
I want a coat knit just for me
from family yarn. I will cobble a basket
from forgotten prayers, lost recipes, walk
through the razed city, gathering
silenced language, forbidden laps. I will climb no ladders,
only rest in the chant of gift-giving tongues,
build a house for my fellows, a generous house,
set the table, places for my ghosts
and time to listen. I will bind myself to mystery,
its flow from narrowed walls into opening.
Let me come home.

# The Dina Letters

### BARBARA F. LEFCOWITZ

1. *My Questions:*
Dear Dina, long dead great-aunt I never met, in my imagination you're riding the Blue Train above the rooftops of Belarus. I think they just called it Russia back then. You're riding over snowfields, that like everything else are tinged blue, even the miasmal fumes from the Pripet Marshes.

You're wearing a blue shawl, a blue kerchief knotted around your thin face whose blue eyes resemble those of my mother. She was named for you. That's a fact. Which means you died sometime prior to her birth, which took place in 1909, another fact. But where and of what you died I'll never know.

Dina, you're riding the Blue Train all the way to America, sixteen years old, your hunched back risen behind you, a loaf of bread so thick and high you must hang your head, lean far forward in your seat, so your breasts, full of desire, brush against your knees.

Nobody sits next to you, none of your many sisters or brothers, not even your dear mother or your father, Jacob. So after tucking the loose ends of your shawl, I seat myself on the wooden plank next to you and ask:

Dina, did you really die in Pinsk, left behind when the family emigrated to America or were you turned back at Ellis Island? Or did you really die on Rivington Street in the Lower East Side?

Were you sometimes happy even though they called you the "Hunchback" and wrung their hands, *vey iss mir*, she'll never have any suitors, an old maid, a burden, a curse, *gott in himmel*, what have we done to deserve this? Excuse my questions; I really want to know you, know the place you came from, the place you came to, the place where you died.

Why did the officers at Ellis Island cross out your name on the passenger manifest, yet stamp you admitted, followed by the scrawled words *Deformity of the Spine*? As if you were a double of yourself. Dina, I can't help thinking about Dinah, defiled daughter of another Jacob.

One hundred years later almost to the day of your ship's arrival in New York, 2/20/1904, I discovered you on microfilm in the New York Public Library on Forty-Second Street. Of course, I'll never know the true, the real story, no matter how often I ride along with you on the Blue Train to . . . much as I hate to say, the Blue Train to your death and soon enough to mine.

So meanwhile, let's gossip and laugh like any sixteen-year-old girls. I'll tell you all the family dirt and you can tell me your secrets. Perhaps you had a lover from the next *shtetl*, a young rabbi, or better yet a firebrand who stayed behind to fight the hooligans, the drunken Cossacks. But I'll spare you word of the wars, the betrayals.

Dina, time's running out, the train is moving faster, away from America, from Europe, the rest of the world. So please hurry and break your silence. Dina. Jacob's daughter with the hunchback and crossed-out name. *L'Chaim!* Sincerely, Your Grand-Niece, Barbara

2. *Her Answer:*

Barbara, or should I call you Basha? Please excuse my simple words. Mama knew Hebrew, Yiddish, a little Russian and Polish, but only the boys were allowed to read and write.

But I hid under the table and pressed inside my head whatever I could hear them learn until my back hurt so much I had to crawl away. Once Papa caught me and beat me. He was drunk from too much slivovitz and praying.

Mama would try to flatten my back with rolling pins and irons. When nothing worked she blamed me and cried. I hardly ever went outside except when everyone was sleeping. In the dark no one could laugh at me, curse me for not being perfect.

Are you perfect? I hope not.

But there were some good things. I didn't have to carry wood and pails through the snow and I had the whole tub to myself, it was only a big tin pan from the milk farm but I could sit there, no one staring at my body. Oh, I had my secret ways, I must—how you say?—confess.

My hands were good so I sewed all the clothes lying on the floor which got cold and damp. At night my hands found all kinds of places nobody knew about except me and the devil—the one who cursed me when I came out wrong from Mama, that's what they all said, even the doctor. Sometimes Papa said I was only good enough to be a *kurveh*—a bad word I think means whore.

Promise you won't tell anyone, but I never believed in any devils, except maybe Izzy Koretsky who had red teeth. No more than I believed in the God that Papa prayed to make me stand up straight—be beautiful like my sisters, your grandma Annie, so quick and smart, little Zelda and *Schaine Fagele*, the pretty bird. I hated her the most. She and Zelda danced on the deck of the ship. All the rich people clapped and gave them candy.

Me? Down with the rats in the stinking dark steerage crying to go home. Mama said sixteen-year-old girls don't cry. Most of them are already married with babies. Maybe in America . . . I'd become a *kurveh*, a whore, just to spite them, but it must hurt bad when men put their things inside you, and I could never lay flat to open my legs enough. Milk and honey, everyone said. America was made from milk and honey. How could they believe such nonsense about a place? A place they had never seen . . .

But the stories never fooled me. Even if that place did exist, for me it was hard enough to walk on earth. I would drown in all that damn milk and honey, trip over the gold on the streets which was probably just dreck from the animals anyway.

When the ship docked in New York on February 20, 1904 it was cold and gloomy. From the little I could see the snow looked gray, like it needed to be scrubbed clean. Not at all like the pure white snow fields of Pinsk. I kept wishing those big blond American soldiers who sent us into an enormous hall . . . ach the noise! the smell of fumes from what they called disinfectant, as if we were full of disease. Much worse than the fumes from the Pripet Marshes. I kept wishing those soldiers and the goyish doctors who also wore uniforms and never smiled would order me to go back home.

Home to where I could listen to the music of splitting icicles and look up at the stars. They said the marshes made people sick, gave them *pinske blutte*, I think it means weak blood, but in the spring long reeds and sometimes wild red poppies sprang up and I could shape the mud to little figures, maybe a golem like in the story Papa once told me. If I dipped my hands deep enough, I'd feel lots of warm things, like when I put my hands inside me, once I found a stuck bird and made its wings free—

If only Mama had not convinced them to admit me, I guess she felt guilty, no, I really think she believed in her heart America would cure me but I hated those goddamn stinking little rooms on Rivington Street, all of us packed like a barrel of herrings with other families, babies crying, such noise, no place to hide.

Sometimes I'd sneak out and walk across the bridge to Brooklyn, have you heard of it? That big silvery bridge, and I'd build myself a little house on someone's fire-escape. Nobody ever noticed me, except one night it got very cold and my coat bulged in back so I couldn't button it. Such a fever I got! Mama wrapped me in rags soaked with hot urine and mustard.

But I refused to get better. I think they were relieved, what a burden I was, maybe more than my back was to me. Thank you for your concern and for taking the time to make me up based on so few facts. It's almost like—how you say?—making up to me something I lost. Almost. —Yours, Dina

# My Indian Bene Israel Home

## Erusha Newman

When I was a child in India, my father was employed by the British, prior to independence, and was required to move from time to time. It wasn't until 1942 that we finally settled in Pune and my large family could establish roots. I had six brothers and four sisters, and it was up to my mother to establish a core around which family life could develop. This core was rich with our Indian Bene Israel holidays.

Years later, in March of 1976, I boarded a flight in Bombay, India, bound for Cleveland, Ohio, to join my brother and mother. What I brought with me from India to my new life in America, more than any worldly possessions, are memories of the Holy Days.

## Shabbat

My mother would light an oil lamp, which consisted of coconut oil in a large glass bowl with a cotton wick. There was enough oil for the lamp to burn until the end of Shabbat. We had a small cotton bush in our front garden and my mother would collect the cotton and make wicks by rolling the cotton on fine bamboo sticks. The lamp was placed on a special table in the corner of the living room and the bowl was used only at Shabbat and our Jewish holidays.

She lit the lamp and then my father led the Shabbat prayers by giving his blessings to each family member, starting with the youngest. Then the family sat around the dining room table, where my father said Kiddush over home-made wine and bread, which was then distributed to everyone.

The wine was made by soaking dry grapes in warm water overnight and then bringing it to a boil the next day. The dry grapes would plump up and be crushed by hand, to extract the juice. Whole wheat flour was kneaded into dough, and rolled out into two thin flat breads, which were then roasted on a griddle until crisp. These were placed in a small bowl containing salt, and kept on a special plate.

After prayers over wine and fruit, my father washed his hands and mumbled a prayer, which none of us could hear, before blessing the two crisp breads. He would hold the two breads in his hand, sprinkle salt on the top one, and break pieces for everyone.

The tradition in Bene Israel homes was to say a prayer over the fruits of the season, one fruit an annual, and one a perennial. After the prayers, we helped mother set the table for dinner—usually chicken curry, chapattis (Indian flat bread), rice, and vegetable.

## Rosh Hashanah

As small children, we looked forward to the High Holy Days, because it meant getting new clothes—fancy and very colorful for Rosh Hashanah, and simple white for Yom Kippur. But as we grew older, the clothes didn't mean much; it was more important to get together as a family.

Special treats, in Bene Israel households, were prepared days before the holidays. On Rosh Hashanah, my mother would prepare an elaborate meal of chicken or fish curry, rice, vegetables, and chapattis.

Every Bene Israel home prepared a special halvah made from wheat gluten, coconut milk, sugar, and saffron. This mixture, about the consistency of milk, was put in a large, thick-bottomed vessel, placed on a hot coal fire and stirred continuously for several hours until it was the consistency of Jell-O. This process was laborious and everyone had to join in the stirring until the desired consistency was reached. Only mother knew when that was and no one could get out of this job. The batter was poured into deep platters (*thalis*) and sprinkled with almonds, pistachios, golden raisins, and poppy seeds. It had to be completely cooled before being cut into squares. My brothers were given the task of delivering the finished product to very close relatives and many friends, who were not necessarily Jewish.

We attended Rosh Hashanah services in our best clothes. The services were held in the Bene Israel synagogue, a long way from where we lived. After services, we returned home to more prayers followed by a delicious meal. Though she lived far away, visiting our grandmother after dinner was a tradition in our family. We walked there with our parents, to get her blessing for the coming year and the years to come. She had all sorts of treats ready for us to devour.

We lived on the banks of the Mulla and Mutha River, which was the only water venue available at which Jews could perform the *Tashlich* ritual of disposing of their sins after Rosh Hashanah. After this Tashlich prayer, friends and relatives would stop by to wish my parents well for the holidays.

## Yom Kippur

A somber holiday. We fasted the traditional twenty-four hours, went to the synagogue, and then broke the fast at home. Everyone in the synagogue wore white clothes, unlike at any other holiday. After an early dinner we attended Erev Yom Kippur services and returned for the morning and afternoon prayers the next day. Since we lived a distance from the synagogue, we stayed on the premises until the evening prayers were over.

On returning home, hungry and exhausted, we looked forward to breaking the fast with family members. This we did with homemade wine, followed by the *puris* and other treats. The *puris* are a type of pastry filled with a mixture of roasted cream of wheat, sugar, sliced almonds and pistachios, golden raisins, poppy seeds, coconut, and cardamom. Here again, the process was very laborious, and everyone had to lend a hand in the preparation of this elaborate treat. Another delicacy was coconut-filled pancakes (blintzes), delicious with lamb or chicken curry.

My older siblings were given the responsibility of making all the pre-fast-breaking purchases of various foods at the local bakery, along with plenty of soft drinks to quench twenty-four hours' worth of thirst. Dinner—prepared after breaking the fast—as the usual: curries, and vegetables with rice and chapattis.

## Sukkot and Simchat Torah

Though we did not build a Sukkah at home, the synagogue had one built—of bamboo, palm and banana leave—and decorated with flowers and fruits. In the center of the sukkah, a *lulav*, made of a lemon with palm leaves, was hung from the ceiling. The synagogue provided snacks and other refreshments for the congregation.

On Simchat Torah we went to the synagogue to enjoy the dancing with the Scrolls. After prayers the congregants took the Scrolls and walked or danced around the *bima* amid loud and deafening chants from the Bible. This would continue far into the evening, until everyone was exhausted and ready to go home.

## Not Just a Memory

Those were the happy times with my family. I continue to light Shabbat candles. I prepare *puris* and halvah. As was the custom at home,

I continue to celebrate the High Holy Days by inviting friends and relatives to enjoy our traditional snacks and Indian food. I continue to transfer my Indian Bene Israel home from my birthplace to my new life in the United States.

# In Your Letter

## Julie Parson-Nesbitt

In your letter you said *Yes, our families wither,*
*get weak, lose members. Families that once were strong,*
*cohesive, alive. It hurts but that's how things*
*must go.* You said *Praying is like poetry:*
*inventions, hopes, dreams.* I didn't believe you.

Prayers were extravagant filigree necklaces
spun out of ornate, incomprehensible syllables,
mysterious and hushed like traffic on far-away highways.
God's praise unconnected to anything else.
Still utterly magnificent.

*Spirituality* arrived later, shrink-wrapped in plastic:
crystals for sale at chain bookstores;
prayers like a personal to-do list for God;
meditation trips to sacred boulders in Mexico
for anyone spiritual enough to afford them.

Suffering does not make you good.
But it tears down everything you thought was true.
I thought my life was a real and ongoing life:
waking up to the bird hum of a child's voice,

the day filled with papers, notebooks, phone calls,
familiar sleep. As if the world were intact,

as if the life I cared about mattered.
I didn't know this lashing anger—
everything lost and destroyed and senseless.
I didn't know this path without breadcrumbs—
dark blue sky above dark blue water.
I didn't know death was my real life.

What people call *good* is just staying alive
in that other place. When you reach someone
in that darkness, any way at all, that's prayer.

Luis, thank you for praying for my sister.
We have limitless capacities for caring,
you tell me in your letter, opening currents
of goodness the way jets release trails of cloud
high above as they break the speed of light.

*For Luis Rodriguez*

# If Only I'd Been Born a Kosher Chicken

## JYL LYNN FELMAN

The problem with my mother's dying is not so much that she died, but that she died without telling me how to make a chicken. If I could make a chicken, the way my mother did, I could have her with me always or so I imagine. In my fantasy, whenever I want to talk to my mother, I go to the kosher butcher or buy Empire frozen if I'm in a hurry, and I cook that chicken until my mother appears alive and well before me. So strong is the smell of the roasting chicken in my mind, that I feel my mother coming into the room this very minute.

My mother washed us both in the same kitchen sink. Only I don't know who came first, the baby or the bird. First, I am on the counter watching, then I am in the sink splashing. My mother washes me the way she washes her kosher *Shabbas* chicken breasts. Slow and methodical, as though praying, she lifts my small right arm; she lifts the wings of the chicken; and scrubs all the way up to where she can not scrub anymore, to where the wing is attached to the body, the arm to the shoulder. Plucking feathers from the freshly slaughtered bird, she washes in between my fingers; toe by toe. Gently she returns my short stubby arms to the side of my plump body, which remains propped upright in the large kitchen sink. I am unusually silent throughout the duration of this ancient cleansing ritual. Automatically my arms extend outward, eternally and forever reaching for her.

The cold wet chicken, washed and scrubbed, sits next to us on the counter. I weigh more than the chicken but as far as I'm concerned we're identical, the chicken and I. Except for our heads and the feathers. The chicken has no head and I have no feathers. But I will have hair. Lots of body hair on this nice Jewish girl that my mother will religiously teach to pluck and to shave until my adolescent body resembles a perfectly plucked, pale young bird waiting to be cooked to a hot crisp, golden brown and served on the same sacred platter as my mother herself was before me.

At thirteen I stand on the bimah waiting to address the entire congregation. I am also upstairs in the bathroom, alone in the terrifying wilderness of my adolescent femaleness. But I stand on the bimah and prepare to chant. On my head is a white, silk yarmulke, held in place by two invisible bobby pins. For the first time in my life, I prepare my female self the exact same way she taught me in her kosher kitchen sink. *Borachu et Adoni hamivorach.* I look out at the congregation of *Beit Avraham.* My mother is crying. I look in the mirror; I inspect my face, my eyebrows are dark brown and very thick. *Baruch atah Adoni hamivorach laolam voed.* I place the tweezers as close to the skin as possible to catch the root, so the hair won't ever grow back. *Baruch atah Adoni, Elhaynu melach haolam . . .* My parents are holding hands as I recite the third blessing in honor of being called to the Torah. And then I begin. Although my haftorah portion is long and difficult I want it to last forever because I love the sonorous sounds of the mystical Hebrew letters. But I am surprised at how much it hurts to pull out a single hair, one at a time out from under my pale young skin. When I reach the final closing blessings my voice is strong and full and I do not want to stop.

The rabbi asks my parents to stand. They are kissing me, their youngest baby girl. But I am surprised at how much it hurts to shape my thick Ashkenazi eyebrows into small elegant, Anglo female arches. Then I remember the ice cubes that she soaks the chickens in, to keep them fresh and cold before the plucking and how I used to watch her pluck out a long, hard particularly difficult feather without a single break. She had special fleishech tweezers, for use in the kitchen only. The congregation sings *Mi chamocha boalim Adoni*. I return to the kitchen for ice cubes wrapped in terrycloth that I hold diligently up to my adolescent brow. *Mi chamocha Adoni nadar bakodesh* . . . Who is like unto thee, O most High, revered and praised, doing wonders? I have no feeling above my eyes, but the frozen skin is finally ready for plucking.

These first female rituals have no prayers as I stand before the rabbi, utterly proud of what I have accomplished. He places his hands above my head, *Yivorech et Adoni* . . . He blesses my youthful passage into the adult community of Jews. Alone in the bathroom my eyes water as I watch the furrowed brow of my beloved ancestors disappear from my face forever. At the exact same moment that I become a Bat Mitzvah I begin the complex process of preparing myself for rebirth into gentility. I complete these first female rites in silence, without the comfort of my mother or a single Hebrew *brocha*. The congregation rises, together we say, *Yiskadel, Viskadesh sh'ma rabo*. Today I am permitted to mourn publicly. I have become a beloved daughter of the covenant, only the covenant is confusing. *Shema Yisrael Adoni echad*, I love my people Israel, but I loathe my female self. Is this what my mother wanted for me? On the occasion of my Bat Mitzvah, my body splits apart and my head becomes severed from the rest of my body, a chicken without a head, a head without a body.

I am balanced precariously between the sink, the toilet, and the cold tile floor. I use my father's shaving cream to hide all traces of the hair growing up and down my legs. I stand in a wide V, and smother my right leg in white foam. My left leg supports my young body while my right leg straddles the sink. Slow and methodical, I scrape the hair off each leg. I have to concentrate very hard so I don't cut myself. Every two minutes I stop to rinse out the thick tufts of hair stuck in the razor's edge. Then I inspect the quality of my work. The finished skin has to be completely smooth, as though there never was any thick brown hair covering my body. Convinced that the right leg is smooth enough, I lower it to the floor. When I am finished shaving the lower half of my body I raise my right arm and stare into the mirror. The hair under my arms is soft and there isn't very much there. At thirteen, I do not understand why I have to remove this hair too. As I glide the razor back and forth, I am aware of how tender my skin is and how raw it feels once all the hair is removed. Rinsing off the now clean space, I notice that the skin is turning red. And when I roll on the sticky, sweet-scented deodorant, it burns. But I lower my right arm, lift my left one and begin again until I am fully plucked and have become my mother's chicken.

She shows me how to remove all traces of blood from the body. After soaking there is salting. But the blood of the chicken accumulates under the wings and does not drain out, into her spotless kosher sink. She roasts each chicken for hours, turning the thighs over and over, checking for unclean spots that do not disappear even in the stifling oven heat. With a single stroke of the hand and a silver spoon, she removes a spot of blood from the yolk of an imperfect egg. First she cracks each one separately into a glass bowl; if the yolk is clear, luminous, she adds it to another bowl. But whenever the blood spreads like tiny veins into the center of the bright yellow ball, she throws out the whole egg.

For my turn, I roll the egg slowly in between my palms; I learn to feel the blood pulsating right inside the center so I don't ever have to break it open. I learn that the sight of red blood on the food Jews eat, is disgusting. Red juice from an undercooked chicken always makes me gag. I stop eating red meat. I eat all my food cooked well done. I do not tell her when I start to bleed. Instinctively I keep my femaleness to myself. I watch her throw out a dozen eggs, one at a time crying at the waste. To spill a drop of blood is to waste an entire life.

When I start to bleed, I keep my femaleness to myself. When she finds out, she is furious. How long? I can not remember. She is hurt. When was the first time? I do not remember. She is almost hysterical but I can not remember. I remember only that all signs of blood on the body must be removed. I do not tell my mother when I begin to bleed. Instead I wrap wads of cotton in toilet paper so thick that no one will ever guess what's inside. I clean myself the exact same way she cleans blood from the chickens in her sink. I soak and I salt. I soak and I salt. For hours at a time. For years I will away my own femaleness. I do not spill for months in a row and then, when I do, it's just a spot, a small speck, easily removed like the red spot floating in my mother's yolk.

Before I am born I float in my mother's yolk and I am never hungry. Soon after I am born the hunger begins. By seventeen I am so hungry I do not know what to do with myself. All I can think about is food and how I can not get enough.

At seventeen I leave the States for Israel. I have to leave. When I arrive *b'eretz* I can not stop eating. I stuff myself the way my mother stuffs her kosher *Shabbas* chicken breasts. I stuff myself with grilled lamb shaved right off a hot, rotating skewer stuffed into warm, fresh pita filled with sautéed onions and lemon juice. In Jerusalem I can not stop eating waiting for the bus to take me to the Turkish Bath House where I crouch in the corner on a low stool, sip steaming Turkish coffee, suck on floating orange peels, and stare at all the naked bodies.

I can not stop eating halvah laced with green pistachios while Mizrachi women with olive skin soak in pools of turquoise water. Slowly as though praying, they unbraid each other's long thick dark hair. Standing in water up to their waists, they comb out the knots. They knead their scalps and foreheads gently, washing their hair in the juice of fresh squeezed lemons. The women soak in silence. Large round bodies move from pool to sacred pool; hot then cold, tepid, and cool. Back and forth. Tall and thin. Brown skin. Torsos dip and soak in swirls of foaming water. Surrounded by the scent of eucalyptus they soak their feet in burning crystals. Bodies in water float through steam.

I want to take my clothes off but I can not stop eating whole figs with date jam spread on fresh Syrian bread, while Sephardic women lie on heated marble slabs and close their eyes. Their breasts sag; sunlight doesn't filter in. Bodies in steam float through air. But I am never full. They drink chilled yellow papaya juice from thin paper cups while cooling their sweating foreheads. I want to take my clothes off but I can not stop eating. Wings and thighs. Breasts and legs. They soak and they salt in pools of blue water. With avocado soap they wash each other's spines and massage their aching muscles. Jewish women bathe in ancient cleansing waters. Wrapped in soft terry-cloth they climb the steps to the roof and begin to eat: plates of humus lined with purple olives, smooth baba ganhouj, and almond macaroons. I can almost touch the sky, sitting on the roof; the Jerusalem sun is hot and strong.

Down below I see the streets of *Meah Shearim*. Narrow sidewalks and small shops. Women concealed within their bodies. Safely covered from head to toe. Orthodox men in black. Praying as they walk. Their eyes never meet. On the street. Their hands never touch. On the street. Women are covered from head to toe.

On the rooftop women eat, naked in the sun; mothers and daughters; sisters. They lounge on cement slabs, laugh among themselves and feed each other grape leaves. But I can not stop eating staring at the street below. Women with children; live chickens squawking. Preparing for *Shabbat*. Men in black hats. Long beards. Everything ordered and prearranged. *Ani Adoni Elochechah*. I am the Lord thy God. The Torah is absolute. I love my People Israel. (I loathe my female self.) I can not stop eating, caught between the roof and the street below. I dream that I am falling, falling to the ground. But I never land. I stay caught forever hanging limb by limb. Caught forever limb by limb. The Jerusalem sun is hot and strong. Burning me at seventeen. Suspended as I am. Between my people and myself.

The suspension makes me crazy as I wander the biblical streets. Where do I belong? The suspension is intolerable. I have no place to go. Every week I visit *Meah Shearim*. Searching not just for my head but my body too. Every Friday I stay with an Orthodox family and light *Shabbas* candles as the sun sets. When I'm in my head my body disappears and then I can not find my Jewish female self. At night I wander back alone from the center of the city, to where I live on *Har Hatzofim*. I search as I walk, staring in the dark, peering into windows looking for my soul.

In the States, I'm in my body, but I can not find my head. At home *b'eretz* I eat my way through the city longing to be whole. With my bus fare I buy a kilo of jelly cookies. I eat as I walk in the dark through villages and urban streets. All I do in Israel at seventeen is eat. I tap a hunger so wide that I do not know what to do. I know that I will have to leave the country. There is no one to tell how hungry I have become because a hunger like this is forbidden.

I have no place to go. I do not know it yet completely. But I fall in love with Israel the way I will fall in love with a woman for the first time. With all my heart and with all my soul. I want to return to the land forever. To live in Meah Shearim. That will save me from my hunger, or so I think and pray. At seventeen, I wander the streets of Jerusalem, terrified at what I know I will grow up to be. But there is no one to tell how hungry I have become because a hunger like this is forbidden. I swallow my passion whole; my body swells until I am so enormous that I have to leave the land I love.

Alone, my mother flies to rescue me on an El Al jumbo jet. But I do not say a word. I have become a *knaydelach*, a dumpling, floating in the soup: a nice Jewish girl who doesn't say a word. But stuffed inside my mother's dumpling, swimming just below the surface is a *vilde chaye* waiting to jump out. A wild beast waiting to get out. My mother takes the window seat staring hard at me, her fat baby girl, drowning in the soup.

Flying back together, I know that I have failed. She doesn't ask and I can not tell her, what exactly happened. That I fell in love. With Sarah and Hagar, and Lot's wife the moment she looked back. She doesn't ask and I can not tell her, what exactly happened.

That I tapped a hunger I did not know I had. I have watched my mother eat and never gain a pound. She can eat and eat, and eat; devour anything in sight, but I never see her body change. I never know what happens to all the food that she consumes. Mine shows on my body, right outside for everyone to see; but the food that she consumes disappears and is impossible to see. My hunger is outside; hers is never seen. Yes, the country's beautiful . . . I did not ever want to leave. And I do not want to cry. Even though I know right inside her dreams for me we can no longer speak.

When we arrive in the States, our covenant begins to break; mother to daughter; daughter to mother. We do not speak the words; but they float between us growing larger day by day. Right after Pesach, like the first signs of spring, I start to grow all my body hair back again. A *Vilde Chaye*. She is mortified. It is so soft. She is horrified. I can't believe I ever shaved it off. A wild beast. I run my hands up and down my legs. And when I lift my arms, she turns her head away. She tells me that my body is disgusting. Not a nice Jewish girl, never seen or heard, who does not say a word. I thought my body was my own. More than her *knaydelach* floating in the soup.

The covenant is broken; I've claimed my body as my own. But the silence floats between us growing larger day by day. What my mother always feared is true. I grow up to be a stunning, raging, wild, forbidden *vilde chaye*. I did not ever want to leave my mother's *Shabbas* table; but in my twenties, she can not set a place for me. I learn to close my eyes, light the candles, say the Kiddush and the *motzi* by myself. But I can not cook her chicken so I can not bring her home to me. And without my mother present, I can not bear to eat her food.

I become a vegetarian even though the food tastes strange and never smells the same. With other *vilde chayes*, I make a seder of my own. We become the red beets sprouting green leaves, sitting where the shank bones belong. We wash each other's hands as we pass the bowl around. But we can not taste our mothers in the soup and in their absence we grow lame. How can I have my mother and myself? For years we barely speak and in her absence I grow tame. Only later do I know that her silence is her shame that she gave birth to me, who let my hair grow back. But I did not ever want to choose my mother or myself. And when we, *d'vilde chayes*, call forth our mothers' names: *Ematanu*, Sarah, Rivkah, Rachel v Leah, it is the first time I say my mother's name out loud.

I know that I have been cast out; that my hunger is the shame of both my mother and my people. My grief is overwhelming that I have no place to go. Either I are heard among the women but never fully seen. Or I are seen among my people but never ever heard. There is no language I can speak as I shake my heads in sorrow that I am not counted too.

But I continue to look back, to remember who I am. *Im eshcahac yerushalayim, t'shchah y'menie*. If I forget (Thee O) Jerusalem, may my right hand lose its cunning. I know my mother's waiting and looking back herself. Through her silence she is praying that I reappear. Through my silence, I am praying for my mother to appear. But to reappear is difficult, not knowing what I'll find. At the *seder* table, with other *vilde chayes* my voice grows strong and clear. I learn that I must speak the words to those who do not want to hear. To my mother and my people, it's hard to speak what they have always feared. That I am your daughter too and can not be forgotten or erased.

The truth is I always was just like I am today. Only I didn't know, it wasn't possible as I was growing up to see any other way. For the longest time I floated in the soup and didn't say a word. Then one day I had to choose to leap right from the bowl. I came to understand that there are those of us who lead the way and those who like to follow. My mother was a follower who gave birth to a leader. This was not easy for my mother or myself. I did not choose to be a leader; it was chosen for me. But what I do not know is if my mother ever felt constrained as I always did; if it was her choice to follow or did she feel, that she had no choice? Perhaps she was afraid to lead, this I'll never know. Yet this is how the cycle flows. In every generation, from follower to leader, *l' dor v dor*. From leader to follower.

All her life my mother didn't understand what it meant to birth a *vilde chaye*. This was my aching disappointment. Before she died, I never had the chance to tell her that to lead like Moses or Deborah is to risk the people's wrath. That to be *a vilde chaye* is to live forever on the edge with your life often at stake. I never had the chance to say out loud that I always needed her. My mother's grief at who I am, is my deepest sorrow. More than anyone on earth, I wanted her to understand and not to be afraid. But this simply wasn't possible; just like me, she didn't know any other way. Sometimes, late at night, when I feel my people's wrath, I wonder, was she right? Is it better not to be ever seen or heard? A dumpling floating in the soup? Sometimes, late at night, with my life out on the edge, I wonder, was my mother right? Is it better just to be a *boobalah*, a nice Jewish girl rather than a *vilde chaye*? I always loved my mother and know that she loved me. The mistake I made is in her chicken that I never learned to cook. From the plucking to the soaking, from the salting to the stuffing, to the removal of the blood, we are bound to language and a common history. From the laws of *kashrut* to the sacred washing of the hands, it is in poultry that we are bound eternal, in our femaleness.

In my fantasy I am born a kosher chicken with my mother's hands holding me. She washes me forever in her large kitchen sink. Cleaning my wings, she tells me not to change a thing. That she loves me just the way I am. On Friday afternoons all her *Shabbas* friends come to see the baby soaking in the sink. They pinch and they poke, laughing at my teeny, tiny *polkies*. As a kosher chicken I'd be blessed by the *shochet* and served on a sacred silver platter with squares of *kugel* by my side to keep me warm. If only I was born a chicken rather than a *vilde chaye*, there would be no painful separation from my mother or my people. I'd be plucked and stuffed then roasted to a crisp, golden brown. Sprinkled with paprika, I'd look gorgeous all the time.

Near the end I washed my mother's hands and feet. She couldn't talk but she let me in that close. As I washed her legs and thighs, we made a silent, fragile peace; she the perfect *balaboosta*, and me, the stunning *vilde chaye*. But in my fantasy, I am born a kosher chicken. I sit forever plumb and round, in the center of my mother's *Shabbas* table. When she lights the candles and closes her eyes, I am there forever by my mother's side. She is there forever, by her daughter's side. We are together, at the *Shabbas* table, sitting side by side.

# My Mother's Roots

## Helen Degen Cohen/Halina Degenfisz

My mother

never taught me to embroider
coarse white tunics
                or weave
garlands of warm chamomile,
never took me to circle dances,
never finished a song, or even a phrase,
never sang, but hummed to herself
hummed and hummed
an entire village
cooked and hummed and the humming

was the sound of the world in darkness

was her own mother humming the beginning
of *Enchanted Fairy Tales, Exquisite Fairy Tales*

her mother like a thick white star come out of the night
to touch her, where she stood sweating, tasting the chicken soup
in the middle of the universe
of a house that would not come together

even as turnips and parsnips awakened
the town, the night the first one went, age two,
her hair black as pearls, humming, halo of pearls, turnips,
humming the soup throughout the house

*Aleph, Bet*, humming, A, B, humming, *offen pripechik*, close by the hearth,
*where the rabbi stood, instructing the children*

as if the gentle white scum, carefully removed, would release
the soup to fragrance and heal the
what and the who can say, when was it
she stopped wearing aprons?

as if the soft steam on the windows
between here & there
were not the steam of a fading locomotive and not
her sisters' breath, celery and carrots
and parsley root—and the leek,
as she smelled it, took up the humming

when I was twelve, then forty, then now,
only a child of the future, not of her home town, not
of the body of the first house where twenty children
were born and died of natural causes while everyone cooked and some
even danced and sang out loud, loud and
haughty in satin and manicured. My
mother's manicured hands
stir, stir & cook, stir

as if she were not dissolving with each
onion, each carrot. She looks at me and smiles and the bits
of humming resume, when was it

I refused to eat her soup?

as if when I sweated to
Russian balalaikas she was not in the shadows to
counterpoint—dancing? dancing?? to steam sweetening and
saddening (she hummed) all the
children behind the walls, the children behind the walls?—
   whatever
happened to the Russian balalaikas?

She hummed. And the
world changed and changed.
Became. Darkened a shade.
Became the world. Or had been
all along. Ask a thousand
mothers who hum, a million.
In Kenya. In the Andes. In Spain.

As if the chalk circle around my feet,
out of which and into which I jumped
with all the children in the world were not
a house breathing a cloying mist

and I wasn't cooking carrots & parsnips & turnips
& onions & celery & chicken & parsley & salt & pepper & sometimes
parsley root, when I could get it, and the vapors
didn't replenish the night
or soften the stars, as I skimmed
the delicate scum, carefully, when was it
I stopped wearing aprons?

# My Iranian Sukkah

## Farideh Dayanim Goldin

Every year after Yom Kippur, my husband Norman and I try to bring together the pieces of our sukkah, our temporary home for a week, a reminder of our frailty as Jews. Every year we wonder where we had last stored the metal frame, the bamboo roof, and the decorations. Every year we wonder about the weather. Will we have to dodge the raindrops and the wind once again this year for a quick *bracha* before eating inside? Will our sukkah stand up? Will there be a hurricane?

I insisted on building a sukkah the first time we had a yard. My husband protested that it would never last in Portsmouth, Virginia, remembering the sukkahs of his childhood and youth in that town, when his father, Milton, struggled to balance the wobbly structure in the more protected area outside the living room. Every year, my father-in-law had to bring it down in the middle of the holiday, fearing that strong winds from one hurricane or another would topple the sukkah against the building, bringing down bricks, glass, and the roof shingles.

In Iran of my youth, we had no such worries. Every year, a month before the holiday, my father ordered four young trees from the town's wood supplier. He made sure they were cut to the exact height and had the two largest branches trimmed in a V, like two hands ready to catch a ball. Nails and screws being forbidden in building a sukkah, the V on top of each tree supported the trunks of narrower ones to shape the skeleton of our sukkah.

My father and uncles worked diligently to tie the supporting beams with sturdy ropes, which again and again they wrapped around the connecting branches, making strong knots. They removed four tiles from the paved yard, dug deep, put the poles in and poured cement around them. Had we had hurricane winds, that sukkah would have remained sturdy and protected against the tall wall that separated us from our Muslim neighbors. We didn't worry about our sukkah coming down. It was sturdy even though sukkahs are supposed to be unsteady, moving to the rhythm of the wind.

It seems that every sukkah my husband and I made in Virginia came tumbling down. We tried different designs: wooden poles set in cinder blocks from the *Jewish Catalog*, four by fours set in holes in imitation of my father's; but none withstood the winds that uprooted them. Once my engineer brothers built the strongest sukkah we had ever had. But as we sat there sipping cardamom tea and cracking roasted watermelon seeds between our teeth, the sukkah tilted and went down in one piece. It held together nicely, and the walls and decorations were still intact, but it was uninhabitable.

We kept building different models of sukkahs. Our latest is a fabricated one bought from a sukkah Web site. It is generic, similar to many other sukkahs that go up in the neighborhood and around the country. It doesn't have the flavor of our sukkahs past, but it has proved to be sturdier although it shakes and loses its roof once in a while to strong winds.

In the city of my birth, Shiraz, our sukkah never came down from a natural disaster. Being very far away from any body of water, we didn't have weather disturbances like Virginia hurricanes. In the desert climate, no one had ever seen our dry river overflow to the city even during unusual storms. Strong winds never came in the fall; the weather was pleasant, sometimes a bit chilly at night under the star-studded sky. We huddled together, all of us who lived in our large communal home: my parents and siblings, my married uncle and his family, my grandmother, a single uncle and another aunt.

Long ago, in another country, another time, my father and uncles competed with the rest of the community, as everyone bragged about their larger sukkahs and their more beautiful walls made of handmade rugs. Every year, a traveling merchant stopped by our house before the holiday with a new supply of kilims, flat woven carpets with geometric designs in the bright colors of the desert mountains streaked with minerals. On the gray bricks that paved our yard, the salesman displayed the carpets like a magical quilt, like Jacob's coat of many colors. And when we examined them closely, lost among the triangles and shooting lines were bits and pieces of flat bread, dates, and long-grained rice from the lunch the village women and their daughters had eaten just a few hours earlier after they had finished tying the last knots on the loom—sitting cross-legged with wool and silk underneath their fingernails. We gladly gave the merchant our old carpets in exchange, happy to purge ourselves of the old, not realizing their value.

My mother complained that her beautiful silk shawls and scarves were being ruined as my father confiscated them to decorate the upper edges of the hanging kilims under the palm leaves of the roof as if the sukkah was a *hejleh*, a bridal canopy. My father couldn't stop smiling as he finished hanging the silk scarves woven with designs of paisleys, cypress trees gracefully bending into the wind, the symbol of our city. Such beauty!

In Virginia, for the walls of our sukkah, my husband experimented with blue tarp that dried quickly after a rain shower but kept the heat in mixed with the smell of plastic. We draped our temporary home with colorful sheets that were weighted down with rain and pinned *shanah-tovah* cards from family and friends in imitation of Norman's past sukkahs, a custom his mother, Florence, remembered and suggested. My parents' cards from their exile in Israel were always the most beautiful, with Hebrew and Persian inscriptions, with roses and singing nightingales shining underneath white and pink glitter, laced with memories of a lost past that I once tried to forget, but now yearn to revive.

In Iran, Sukkoth was fun for us children. We made conical containers with construction paper and cheap glue, and filled them with a mixture of ground roasted chickpea flour and sugar—lots of sugar. After the holiday, as we watched the men dismantle the sukkah, we tore the tips of the cones to enjoy their grainy sweetness with a cup of jasmine tea. We competed with other cousins in making the nicest decorations: lanterns made with sticks and colorful strings, clusters of pomegranates still clinging to their branches and leaves, small round watermelons, boiled eggs painstakingly crisscrossed with hand-painted strings, quince that would end up in a stew with tomatoes and yellow plums, and unripe persimmons that slowly softened as the holiday progressed—their flesh gooey, bright orange, and mouthwatering—a sukkah demolition treat.

In Virginia, after the holiday ended, there were no treats from the sukkah for my daughters when they were young. The plastic grapes and apples went in a basket for another year. The chain made of construction paper, of hours of laughter and fun, sat limp and colorless on top of the pile of pine tree branches that we had used for *sekhag*, a roof covering that oozed and dropped brown and green needles on our plates of eggplant stew over basmati rice.

Over the years, I tried to emulate my Iranian sukkahs past. I taught my daughters how to string fruit that rotted halfway through the holiday and dropped on white shirts, well-groomed hair, and flowery silk skirts as we entertained friends with sweet round challahs and honey. Apples, red, green, and yellow, adorning our sukkah like precious stones, attracted bugs and bees that stung a little girl with green eyes and honey-color hair—a little girl my daughter Yaeli had invited along with her Hebrew Academy class to stop by on their sukkah-hopping journey to munch on candy and chips.

For the school visit, my daughters had made sure I wouldn't serve something so terrible as fruit and a plate of roasted chickpeas and raisins. It was bad enough that in their lunch boxes they found plain yogurt mixed with grated cucumbers and crushed dried mint instead of the sweet fruit yogurts their friends devoured. Their classmates stared as my daughters unwrapped pita stuffed with meat and potato patties, scallion and cilantro, and dates instead of cookies and candy. The girls loved the food but their friends noticed their differences, their hybrid blood that set them apart. Therefore, for the second-grade visitors, I removed from the sukkah the roasted watermelon and squash seeds, the rice cookies sprinkled with rose water. Instead, I served them caffeine-free sodas and store-bought chocolate chip cookies that I covered with autumn-color napkins. But the bees arrived in their yellow armor, usurping the place, oblivious to the children who, screaming and crying, surrendered the sukkah.

We soon learned to replace the pomegranates, persimmons, and quinces with little fall gourds and Indian corn, produce I had never known in my Iranian life, but which didn't entice the bugs. In Iran, we had saved the pomegranates from our sukkah to mix with the *khoroset* for Passover, carrying our Jewish life from one holiday to the other. In America, although I buy them in the fall before Sukkoth, they appear as guests only in the sukkah, to be saved in the refrigerator for the spring holiday of Passover.

For years, I struggled to transport my childhood memories of the holiday to my adopted homeland, to share them with my children who dream of visiting Iran as they have become young women. When I told my daughters of the colorful sukkahs that went up all around Shiraz in the secluded ghetto, behind the privacy walls of Jewish homes, and in my own backyard in a Muslim neighborhood, they made plans to travel to Iran. They made plans to visit the ancient cemetery in Shiraz to pay respect to the tombs of their paternal great grandparents, whose eyes follow them from the picture frames by the Shabbat candles at home. They made plans to visit the tombs of Esther and Mordechai in Hamedan, my mother's hometown. Building their dream travels, they turned to me, "Why didn't you teach us Farsi?" they asked. I regretted that by distancing myself from my heritage, by wanting to discard my Iranian past for many years, I had denied both my children and my parents the pleasures of verbal communication.

I am amazed that my daughters have created such unrealistic dreams to connect with my country of birth, the country I had so desperately tried to escape, to forget. I tell them not now. I fear that my childhood home will be inhospitable to them because they are women, because they are Jewish, because they are American, because they are my children. Children of writers cannot go to a country where words are criminal. Instead I feed them Persian rice, stews with lamb shanks, dill, and cilantro. I add a touch of nostalgia, a pinch of history. I feed them my memories of a lost home.

With our children grown and gone these days, I decorate the sukkah by myself. The walls are pretty, factory-built with Hebrew lettering, recalling our forefathers, Abraham, Isaac, and Jacob—not our foremothers, Sarah, Rebecca, Rachel, and Leah. So I conjure their names. Let the women not be forgotten.

Sukkoth meant hard work for the women in my Iranian family. Although they didn't get along, they had to cook together, carry the food outside, and the dirty dishes back inside. My memories of the holiday are as much about the aroma of my mother and grandmother's food as they are about the construction of the sukkah. And I regret that I have no stories of sukkahs in the shtetels of Kiev and Ponovitz, the birthplace of Norman's grandparents, to tell my children. I cannot re-create his paternal grandmother, Fanny's, homemade gefilte fish made from the carp in the bathtub. I don't know what Norman's maternal grandmother, Jenny, made, but I have tried to revive their memories. I make corned beef with brown sugar and mustard glaze. As we enjoy its spicy sweet flavor in our sukkah, I tell them it is grandma Florence's recipe, which I serve with basmati rice, dill, black-eyed beans, and braised cabbage, my mother, Rouhi's food. We sit in the sukkah and compare: Who would like *gondi*, dumplings made of roasted chickpea flour, ground chicken and cumin, my maternal grandmother Touran's favorite? Who prefers *koofteh*, meatballs with herbs and rice, the way Khanombozorg Tavous, my paternal grandmother made them? To remember Fanny, I make gefilte fish from the frozen loaves (not so bad for a Mizrakhi woman). Our stomachs full and cozy, our spirits high, our hearts warm, we know we are at home in our shaky sukkah even if many others are not.

My father stopped building sukkahs over a quarter a century ago. Sometimes it is hard to believe that the Iranian Revolution is that old. The image of an angry man with black turban and bushy eyebrows is still fresh even though Ayatollah Khomeini has been dead for years. The image of American hostages with wide bands over their eyes, hands cuffed, is still vivid.

The chaos at Mehrabad airport in Tehran as my family rushed to escape Iran on one of the last El Al flights to Ben Gurion still haunts my father's sleep. Vivid nightmares wake him up in the middle of the night. He screams incoherent words, sweating, thrashing. My mother shakes him, "Wake up, wake up." He sits in bed jabbering and trembling: they have come to arrest him; they have called the police with lies; they have taken away his home; they are tearing apart his farm and orchard. We never know who "they" are: the government, the enemies in the community, the envious villagers, and, of course, ever-present, daunting fate.

My father had built his sukkah strong, his house even stronger, and his business indestructible. Everything was built carefully, the house, the farm. The foundation of his life had been put together, slowly, thoughtfully, methodically. He had invested all he had in the land, convinced that it would be hospitable. He had made the earth friendly, removed the stones, dug a deep well, and watered the dusty unyielding land. Against all odds, he had made the Iranian desert bloom with flowers and apricot trees. He had built a poultry farm in Shiraz out of a dream shaped during his trip to an Israeli kibbutz. He fed the city with more chickens and eggs than they had ever seen—not just scrawny chickens that came from someone's backyard, not the two eggs you had to beg the grocer to put in a corner of your chador just to find that they had become rotten on their way from some village to the store. My father had made the impossible a reality. He had tamed the land by encircling it with a protective wall that shielded the top soil from the spring floods that came roaring down the mountainside. He had built a house of stones and bricks; he had built a sukkah that took hours to dismantle. And they all disappeared in a puff of the Revolution, worse than a storm, worse than a hurricane, unpredictable and fierce. He lost everything.

I think that maybe a sukkah should rock and sway with the wind. A sukkah should lose its roof and surrender the protection of its inhabitants to the rain or the sun. I think that a sukkah should crush and fall to pieces once in a while. I think that my father became too attached to the land. Switching his business from being a goldsmith to a farmer, he wanted to forget that Jews have always lived on shaky grounds; that a Jewish home is ephemeral even in lands that seem secure.

My father lost his home and because he has not found it yet, neither have we, his children. Of course we have our own homes, our own families, our spouses and children—but we are always insecure in our hearts.

I felt personally attacked on September 11, 2001. Irrationally, I insisted that we should pack and leave. This time, however, the escape route wasn't so clear. The world Jewry has found a cul-de-sac in America. This is our last stronghold.

Ironically, my siblings and I have married Americans who are strongly rooted in this culture, who have long forgotten the tyranny and pogroms their grandparents struggled to leave behind in Eastern Europe. Our spouses are outraged when Iranian Jews in America must report to the immigration office because they are from a country within "the axis of evil." Yet the situation isn't as personal to them as it is to us who were born in Iran, who experienced discrimination, who even feared for our lives. How can the Iranian Jews explain to the authorities that they are in a state of limbo? Homeless, without a country, will they be sent back to Iran to face false charges of treason and spying for America and Israel just because they are Jews, just because they might have visited Israel, just because they escaped to America? Or should they break the law and not report until the storm passes? Can they ever find HOME, where they don't have to worry about their accents, about JEW or IRAN stamped on their passports, where their breath, smelling of *ghormeh sabzi*, herb stew, fresh limes, and raw spring onions, would be as pleasant as the breath of another smelling of chocolate? Our spouses sometimes don't feel the pain as deeply as we do; time has eroded the memory of their grandparents' fears, replacing it with the American promise of freedom and equality.

My husband does sometimes conjure his Ashkenazi ancestors. He reminisces about Grandma Fanny, who at age fourteen left Kiev in steerage, never to see her mother again. Once when Norman was a teenager, the same age as his grandmother when she left home behind in Russia, he and his siblings took her to see "Fiddler on the Roof." To their chagrin, Fanny jumped from her seat as the Cossacks attacked, screaming, "I REMEMBER! I remember those mamzerim, those . . ." The grandchildren were horrified, and tried to pull her down, "Grandma, sit!" And when she wouldn't, they became terse with her the way one disciplines a child: "STOP IT!" At the same time, they were relieved that that audience didn't understand the expletives uttered in Yiddish, a language they didn't understand themselves because Fanny didn't teach it to her children, or maybe it was easier to erase it in order to forget the old country.

My children are proud of me for having written a memoir, for being an author. They brag about me, but I know that when their friends and co-workers get excited about my book and want to purchase it, my children's pride is mixed with just the tiniest bit of apprehension. I know that a small voice inside wishes Mom had written a happier story, not something so private, not something so dark.

I am lucky to have had enough command of the English language to record a tiny portion of Iranian Jewish life. Still, I wonder if the memory will prevail, if my grandchildren and their children will remember my stories.

To make the children laugh, Norman used to mimic his Russian grandmother's accent. "If you misbehave," he used to tell our youngest, Rachel, "do you know what you'll have for dinner?" With a twinkle in her eyes, with a grin showing two missing teeth, our daughter would reply, "Vater and a toot-peek!" Water and a toothpick indeed. Will my grandchildren remember me for my accent, for my mispronunciation of th's and w's? Will they remember and laugh in good humor about the fact that I can never remember where to add "the" and where not to? Or will they also remember *my* story, my parents and my grandparents' stories; the stories of the Iranian Jews?

I wrap these memories, happy and sad, new and distant, in sweetness of baked beets and turnips, the aroma of dill and cilantro, the pungent flavors of cardamom and cumin, the yellows and oranges of turmeric and saffron. I share them with my oldest daughter Lena as we chop and sauté, as we caramelize and braise.

And to keep reminding myself of past sukkahs, in order not to forget Shiraz myself, I planted pomegranate trees in our tiny yard. When one finally gave fruit this year, I cut a cluster with leaves attached. Before storing them in the refrigerator, I took them to visit our Web site-purchased sukkah, which Norman built and I decorated.

This coming Passover, the mixture of walnuts, apples, and wine will be a reminder of the mortar our ancestors were forced to work with in Egypt; of our hardship, bondage, homelessness. When the earth rejuvenates itself this spring, the pomegranate seeds will glitter like rubies in the thick brown paste, reminding us also of the promise of freedom, of our hopes for a safe homeland.

# Home for Thanksgiving

### Rachel Goldin Jinich

My great uncle, "the quadruplets" came to visit over Thanksgiving. With his olive skin and thick accent, my uncle seems to be a citizen of many countries and at the same time a man without a home. This is especially evident in his name, or rather his four names: Manucher, Menasheh, Robert (pronounced with a French accent), and Bobby. He does not always carry the name given to him by his parents, a name chosen carefully at birth maybe to keep alive a departed family member, a great grandfather, a significant ancestor, or maybe just a biblical figure. Instead, like many others in my extended family, his names represent a series of departures and arrivals. *Manucher, amu-ye-man Irani-eh*. Manucher is my Iranian uncle. *Menshashe ze-hoo ha dod-sheli me-yisrael*. Menasheh is my Israeli uncle. Robert is his "official" American name. Bobby is what he calls himself.

My uncle's multiple identities are in fact an accurate representation of my family as a whole. Like Manucher/Menasheh/Robert/Bobby, each family member has a distant shared past that was disrupted in a sometimes volatile political atmosphere of the Middle East. Although a few remained in Iran, many made *aliyah* to Israel in order to escape anti-Semitism and the perils of the Iranian Revolution of 1979. Many family members found a home in Israel, but others discovered that they were still second-class citizens as Mizrakhim, as Middle Eastern Jews. Therefore, they switched countries again to search for their fortunes in America. Consequently, my Iranian side of the family was dispersed both spatially and linguistically.

My quadruple uncle is a good example. Being born in Hamedan, a central city in Iran, and the burial site of Esther and Mordechai, his family moved to Tehran when anti-Semitism became unbearable. Although still a child, he retained his Hamedani accent, which set him apart in the capital. In his new hometown, he was a constant target for Muslim teenagers, who taunted and attacked him in the narrow alleyways leading from school to his house in a poor neighborhood. Life becoming unbearable once again, the family immigrated to the little town of Kiriat Sharet in Israel to live among other Iranian immigrants. My uncle quit school and worked in a factory where an accident severely burned and disfigured his hand. Facing a dead-end life, he moved to New York City, where he worked with Japanese and Spanish customers, picking up the basics of each language, never speaking one fluently. Today, he speaks these various languages he has adopted on his many life journeys with a thick accent and an awkward body language that is sometimes hard to understand. However, he is a great communicator when on a dance floor. As he moves his body to the rhythm of Iranian, Latin, Israeli, or hip-hop music, he is timeless. He crosses the boundaries of culture and language with movement.

My great uncle is the same age as my mother. That's why I call him uncle and my mother doesn't. They lived in two different cities, and when Manucher became Menasheh by immigrating to Israel, they didn't see each other for many years. My mother too is an immigrant. She left Shiraz, Iran, thirty years ago, which explains why my family has mashed potatoes and *polo*, saffron rice with cranberries, barberries, and pistachio at Thanksgiving. She serves turkey and quince stew, and, for dessert, pumpkin pie and *paludeh*, frozen sweet noodles. Leave it to my family to turn an "All-American" holiday such as Thanksgiving into a display of culinary diversity.

Other family gatherings as well can turn into a survival of the most trilingual. To navigate through the multilingual conversations in English, Farsi, and Hebrew, knowing one or two languages is often inadequate. At our Thanksgiving table, English is spoken with Hebrew accents; Hebrew is spoken with Farsi accents, and so on. Over the years I have become accustomed to explaining the origin of my dispersed family to others, and I have also developed an innate connection to people from other parts of the world, who, like myself, have complex cultural identities. My Persian heritage is a large part of who I am. My multicultural family has instilled in me a deep respect and admiration for cultural preservation and tolerance. Different names, languages, and cultures do not hinder familial closeness. Barriers are lifted through shared customs, kisses on both cheeks, adept linguistic acrobatics, and always food that is rarely prepared the same twice.

The oldest members of my Iranian family compare their torn identities to the biblical dispersion after the fall of the Tower of Babel, and often voice their despair at what sin they might have committed to warrant such punishment. But the second generation immigrants, like myself, who have not experienced the bitterness of exile and refugee status, enjoy the best of the Iranian, American, and Israeli cultures. We know our parents made sacrifices by leaving familiar places in order to make our lives sweeter than theirs.

I was born into a cross-cultural environment, to an American father and an Iranian mother. Through their joy of embracing diversity, I have experienced the world thus far. Through my extended Jewish family, through my mother and her quadruplet uncle, I know that home is not a house with curtains on the windows and a car parked outside; it is not just a land that one can call his or her country. In all the Jewish wanderings, home is a place carried in the heart of a family.

# At Home in Shabbat

## Arlene Hisiger

I am a descendant of the tribe of Levi, whose members, unlike those of the other tribes of Israel, were not allotted a parcel of the Holy Land as an inheritance. Instead, they were instructed by Moses and Aaron to elevate themselves above the limits of the corporeal world, to become vehicles of blessing for the nation of Israel. It is for this reason, I believe, that home for me is more a state of mind rather than a concrete location. The sheltering embrace of a spiritual haven is expressed in the sparks of individual deeds and observances.

As a little girl I would observe my mother lighting the Shabbat candles and although I didn't fully comprehend the significance of my mother's act, I sensed that it caused a change in the spiritual climate surrounding her. However, it wasn't until years later, after my mother's passing, as I lit the Shabbat candles surrounded by my own family that I began to appreciate the power of that seemingly simple ritual. As I closed my eyes in preparation for reciting the *bracha* (blessing) that would usher in Shabbat, my mother's image would appear before me. I watched as she inhaled deeply and in the exhale of impassioned prayer, with her hands waving in circular motion, she thrice beckoned the glow of the Shabbat candles to penetrate the week gone by and pierce the dull layers of the workaday week and nullify its negative influence.

I was struck by the enormous power that my mother, and indeed all women have who kindle Shabbat candles. It occurred to me that with the act of kindling the Shabbat candles, a woman assumes mastery over time (not unlike the biblical leader Joshua, who commanded the sun to stand still in the sky over Givon so that he might complete Israel's battle with the Canaanites). By illuminating the Jewish home with the Shabbat candles, a woman affirms spirituality over corporeality. For me, kindling the candles is meaningful because it presages the sacred space of Shabbat, my supreme Home.

My son was born by Caesarean section at a time when it was not unusual for women to remain in the hospital for several days. As it turned out, I developed a fever and needed to remain in the hospital for a full week, which meant that I would spend Shabbat away from home in the sterile (in every sense of the word) hospital environment. The prospect of being away from home on Shabbat dampened my already shaky spirits, though they lifted immeasurably when my husband appeared with a set of travel candlesticks and a pair of candles. Suddenly, it appeared that the gulf between heart and home was bridgeable. And, as I lit the candles in the privacy of my room and softly sang Shalom Aleichem, a kabbalistic prayer composed to welcome Shabbat, to my newborn son, I realized that like the *mishkan*—the portable temple that accompanied the Israelites through their forty-year trek in the wilderness—sanctuaries could have flexible borders.

I vividly recall another instance when I immediately felt at "home." The Shabbat *shacharit* (morning prayer) service at the *kotel* (Wailing Wall) in Jerusalem had just concluded. My husband and I were making our way home when an elderly gentleman tugged at my husband's sleeve and implored us to join him in kiddush—a small repast, usually consisting of various cakes, cookies, wine, and, at times, whiskey or schnapps—that follows the recitation of the kiddush, the prayer sanctifying the Sabbath day.

In addition to us, this gentleman had graciously invited other worshipers to join him. It was only when we reached the table where he had set out his scant offerings of figs, packaged cookies, and wine that I realized how indigent this gentlemen was. The warmth with which he summoned his guests to the kiddush table and the joy with which he served us was an ethical lesson par excellence. His actions resonated deeply with me. Clearly, his invitation was unencumbered by vanity, pride, or artifice. His purpose was not to impress those gathered around him with the surfeit of his material wealth. Rather, he was a man with a mission that emanated from a pure spiritual source, and his mission brought me home.

Perhaps one of the more unlikely homes that I experienced was in Manila, in the Philippines. My husband and I were traveling on business throughout the Far East and had resigned ourselves to a Shabbat dinner of canned tuna and local fruits when we encountered a Jewish businessman residing on the same hotel floor. This man, a well-seasoned traveler, had packed delectable meats and gourmet items from the "old country" and he insisted that we join him and his son-in-law at his Shabbat table. That evening, as we sat together around the table that was resplendently arrayed in white Shabbat finery and crowned with glistening candles, our voices blended in ancient *zemirot* (Shabbat songs), harmonies that transported us to sacred space, beyond the constraints of time and place, to an ancestral haven.

# Learning the Language

### Tracy Koretsky

On that first day, we have no words. We make silent choices of chairs; the dark curly haired man heads straight for the window, the tiny Asian woman prefers the seat near the door. I want the center, and, because I'm the first to arrive, I can have it. I've come early to take a placement exam which I've left almost blank. What I do answer is generally incorrect. In fact, the only phrase that I can say well is, *"Bonjour, parlez-vous anglais?"* This is more fluent than most. We are the beginners.

We follow the models our *professeur*, Andrianne, writes across the board. "I am called (a name). I am (a nationality)." Pedro is Mexican, Valentine, Brazilian, Ole, Norwegian, Tee-Jah, Korean, Sharon, British. At my table, conversing in a steady but quiet current of what I think to be Hebrew, are Yoav, the Israeli, and Jueda, the Syrian. All eyes fix on the chalked introductions; all mouths recite mindlessly, ignorant but hungry.

We progress. We can say what we do. We are students and teachers, ministers and artists, businesspeople and diplomats. Our limitations frustrate us; how can we really explain? Yoav, for example, cannot even pronounce the word for his profession: *eclairarist*. He does lighting for the Israeli cinema—read: chronically unemployed. Mostly, he cares for his infant daughter.

Jueda is a professor of Arab.

"But what do you teach?" Andrianne coaxes twice in French.
"Arab."
"Oh. Okay. Well, next."

Yoav has a habit of standing too close, breathing his ever-present break-time cigarette in my face. "Why you come here?" he says.

I explain again, slowly, in French.

"Talk English already. What? English not good enough for you?"

So I explain a third time, slowly, in English. Passing an exam in French translation is the only obstacle between me and a master's degree in art history. After two years of miserable underachievement in university French, landing in this spoon-fed class only proves that I have used my student loan wisely. Immersion language is the fast track; everybody says so. Yoav squints at me over his smoke, Bogart-style. "You know what I do if I go to America?" he asks. Then, without waiting for my answer, he says, "I never go. If I go to America," he says, patting his chest, "I get off airplane. I kiss the ground."

I know the stories. Every American Jew knows the stories. My ancestors, when the world was a still black-and-white photo, emerged from the dim steerage of huge gray ships, slung their torn bundles across their shoulders, and shielded their eyes from the blinding brightness that was America. And before they stood in the long lines, before they had their teeth scrutinized and their scalps checked, before their names were changed to simple, clean, unthroaty American consonants, they knelt. They knelt and kissed the ground of freedom.

There is a unit on regional cuisine. In French cultural studies this precedes Molière, Flaubert, and the Revolution. We examine small photos featuring cookbook presentations of daring specialties and make sentences saying what we would like for lunch.

Andrianne asks Yoav if he likes escargot.

"I cannot know," he tries to say. "I am kosher."

Andrianne doesn't understand so they both look at me. My hard work had been paying off, and I have become the unofficial class translator. Yoav begins to tell me what being kosher means but I put up my hand to silence him. I explain. Later he asks how I know.

"*C'est évident, n'est-ce pas?*" I respond.

"You?" he asks, then several more times, "You? You?"

Yoav moves to sit next to me. He talks constantly. Every time Jueda shifts, I must know it, everything she says as well. He loves when she is wrong.

"Look how she shout out answers," he protests. "She must always have first the answers."

"We all yell out the answers," I say. "And you're right; it is annoying. Why don't we stop?"

He stabs his pencil on my open page. "You miss point. She does not shout answers always—only when it is my chance to be right."

I am skeptical and must look it.

"You have heard the word *gleibschtack*?" he asks.

"*Gleib* . . . ?"

"Yes. It mean the bag for the back with everything for battle. Every morning the Arab soldiers do exercises and they say, 'Captain, do we do exercises today with *gleibschtack*?' and the captain always say 'Yes.' Always they must be ready for battle. This is Jueda. She is ready."

Jueda stops me in the hall at break, too shy to meet my eyes. In French she says, "I do not know *la Louvre*."

My American enthusiasm froths. Only the biggest, the best, the most famous, I spill. She nods, unimpressed. As she thanks me politely, I become suddenly sad that this woman will never see the great repository of Western devil genius, never even visit the treasures of her own country torn away in pillages.

I look back at her gentle smile. I can see that she thinks I am the one who should be pitied.

Yoav overhears and laughs. "See how ignorant?" he says. "She knows nothing."

"Yoav she is a young woman, and a professor." After all, that's my goal too. If I have learned anything as a Jew, it is that there is no nobler endeavor.

"A professor of Arab," says Yoav, pointing at me, "is nothing. You must only to repeat back."

A week later, fed up, I hiss at him. "Look, if you don't want her to yell out the answers, tell her not to. She speaks Hebrew perfectly well."

"I will not tell her. She is my enemy."

I roll my eyes.

"You tell her," he says.

"What am I? The United Nations?"

"You don't understand," he says. "She is not just my enemy. She is not just enemy of Jew. She is *Jihad*. She is enemy of world."

I'll admit, a chill runs through me at that word. I too have been taught to fear it. I look across the room at the enemy of the world and am startled by the mild blue eyes returning my gaze. She smiles.

Since the word is not in the *American Heritage Dictionary* that I have brought from home, I take the metro to W. B. Smith's, the English-language bookstore, and comb the reference section. At last I find it. *Jihad*: a holy war against infidels; a crusade. Now, how can a person be a holy war against infidels?

Okay, so if I'm an ambassador, I'll be an ambassador. I sit next to Jueda. We both know enough French now to have a pleasant little conversation. She wants me to know that, beneath her scarf, her hair is the same color and length as mine. Then we talk about husbands and children. She wonders why I am not married when I am close to thirty. I tell her that we tend to wait a little longer in the United States. She nods, as if reminded of something she already knows. She reaches for her dictionary. "Oui, égoïste."

I am stunned. Could she be saying something else? I reach for my dictionary and search: égoïste—a selfish person.

"You are wrong," I tell her in French. She returns my gaze with a smile as patient as that of a mother whose child tells charming and fanciful lies. Oh, what difference can it make? In French I say, "That word is pronounced with long 'e's."

At break, Yoav pulls me back into the classroom. He is so furious I must lie and tell him I joined Jueda so I could prevent her from yelling out the answers.

"You say you are Jew," he says, bringing his face close to mine.

"That's because I am."

"You say, 'Yes teacher, I like escargot.' " He does this in falsetto, batting his eyes.

I see the point but pretend I don't. "Um-hmm."

"Why do you not be kosher?"

"I don't think it's necessary anymore. I—"

"What you mean? You don't eat?"

"Pork was dangerous then, Yoav," I say. "People didn't cook it properly and they died. Milk was not pasteurized. These were health laws. A religion creates laws to keep its followers healthy..."

"A religion! A religion! God make laws. God! And you must follow or you are not Jew."

"Now wait just—"

"You are no Jew," he shouts. "No Jew."

My mother is defiant. For one thing, she went to college. This despite the tears of her immigrant mother who feared a lonely old age and a path of wickedness would befall her daughter. My mother loves to tell me this, to tell me how far she has come and hint at how far I may go. My mother loves to put cheese on a juicy pink burger. In my family's house, we still show proudly the heavy brass Sabbath candlesticks. They are pillars atop the mantelpiece, shrouded in dust.

That afternoon, I touch my camera. Why have I brought it? For more than two months, I have not carried it on my afternoon explorations, fearing it would mark me as a tourist. I remind myself that I want these pictures for my mother. I have come to one of the city's oldest streets, the *Rue des Rosiers*. For two and a half centuries, Jews, many even today wearing the traditional black hat and curling forelocks, have fled from persecution here, to the narrow tenements lining this still-cobbled street. I am almost afraid to make the turn onto it, afraid that I will not belong there, equally afraid that I will.

The first store to catch my eye is a cramped, chaotic nest of books and magazines—Yiddish or Hebrew; they look the same to me. I step inside the dimly lit space and browse. I am disappointed that, except for a few photographs, everything seems to be essentially unillustrated, and of course, I don't understand a thing. Still, I pick up some of the books, sort of weigh them in my hand, mildly surprised that the pages feel new and fresh. The proprietor, an obviously wigged lady, comes toward me. I excuse myself in French, and tell her I am just looking. I have to repeat myself twice, for her French is poor.

Back on the street, I am drawn to another window crowded with beautifully worked metal objects. I recognize *mizuzas*, the small cases containing a bit of Torah that some Jews hang in their thresholds to bring blessings to all who pass through. I recognize too, the nine-cupped candelabras used at Hanukkah and the tall brass Sabbath candleholders. But that is all I recognize. And there are so many more things in the window, whole classes of objects for which there is surely a use, but not one that I'll ever know.

I continue on, window to dim and dirty window, the experience repeating itself at the dry goods store, even a place selling nothing but differently shaped candles. It is like a museum in a way, just like another afternoon spent wandering and wondering about things made for a people as far away as time and as forgotten.

My father often tells this story: When the Poles began to push rural Jews into special city ghettos circled by high, locked walls where they frequently died of starvation and cholera, my great-grandfather did not wait for his invitation. He sold everything, then begged his family for more so that he could book passage on an oceangoing ship and a train ticket to a place called Baltimore. He promised his mother and father and sisters too that he would send for them when he had found his fortune in America.

Now the way my father likes to tell it, this young man, Ishmael Alecheim, was not even in America for two days before he'd found himself standing bewildered and hungry on a Baltimore street corner, looking greedily at the window of the first bakery whose signs were in a language he recognized. But though he was hungry, he knew he was not hungrier than his own mama in Poland. And so, his head light, stomach grumbling, he walked on.

The fat baker saw this and was moved. He left his store and stopped my great grandfather Ishmael Alecheim.

"You are a greener!" he said in English. My father pronounced this like "chrener," deep from the back of his throat, and always said it more than once for dramatic effect. And still not understanding, but at least hoping he might be fed, Ishmael Alecheim followed the fat man, who indeed, filled his belly and let him sleep. When he awoke, more people came to see the chrener. They helped him find a room, a tailor to cut for. He married his second cousin and brought one sister over before the Nazis rose to power.

It is not French that floods from the crowded cafés, nor the Yiddish I remember my mother speaking to her parents, but whatever the language, it is spoken while waving one's arms. I choose a table in a corner, anticipating borsht, whitefish, kishke, and tsimmes. I crave the kind of food my mother prepared the two times a year when she wanted us to eat like Jews; the food that made me feel my family had a history larger and more important than the life I knew. I am surprised. I can have falafel, tabouleh, or goat's milk cheese. There are hummus and grape leaves and filo dough pies. Perhaps I've chosen badly. Perhaps this restaurant is popular for its difference.

I escape and continue on, this time taking more care with the posted menus. One after the next, they are all the same, all brimming with men and the smell of a coffee more spicy than French roast. I come to a large place, glassed-in and expensive seeming. Its name is Goldstein's. Surely here, I think, and head inside.

Not until I am handed a menu do I notice that the establishment's name has changed: L'Algers. Why of course, Algeria! I had read about an influx of Algerian Jews, but why here? Why now? What does it mean to be a Jew in Algeria?

The food is so good that I linger and by the time I've finished, the sun is setting, the sky thickening with clouds. I know I should crowd into the metro before the rain comes, but I like it here, in this transported piece of Algeria, a wandering Jew in the New World. Just one drink, I decide, just one to celebrate the wide world and I will be on my way. But what do they drink? I move to the bar and study the offerings, by now wise enough to expect nothing. When there are no bottles of syrupy sherry, I am, frankly, relieved. What I do see is French, an almost definitively Parisian bar. I order my favorite—pastis—the drink that made the eyes of Degas's drifters bleary and soft. I watch as the barkeep pours; it is not a common brand. Then I notice the six-pointed star, the familiar capital "K."

"It's kosher!" I say out loud, in English.

The barkeep looks up, surprised. *"Bien sûr,"* he says.

I raise my glass to him, and drink a silent toast to a people—my people—who forced to call new lands home, take from them, and give to them, and finally, make them their own.

"You tell teacher you go to Orsay on Saturday." Yoav has waited outside the building in the rain to ambush me.

"Yep," I say, opening my umbrella and beckoning him beneath it. "It's half price."

His breath is hot on my face. "God say you must keep Sabbath holy." He is ready to pounce.

"And I did," I say, "in my own way."

His curls stick to his head, his hands ball into fists. "You must go to synagogue." It is almost a threat. A storm is gathering, the summer is coming to an end, and somehow walking away is not enough this time. I have come here to master a second language, and not just any language, but the language of diplomacy. Yet before this man and his cherished intractability, I know no words that he will ever, can ever, hear. In the end, it is an Englishman I quote: "There are more things in heaven and earth, Horatio, than are dreamt of in your philosophy."

And with that, I do walk away, this time for good. I never return to my language class. Instead I spend my final days in Paris wandering the Louvre, finding God in evidence through the gifts of humanity, preparing myself to share them.

# When We Are Born
# We Are Given a Golden Tent
# and All of Life Is the Folding
# and Setting Up of the Tent

### Edith Altman

The recent death of my father pushed me to return to the place where he was made a victim, an experience that characterized his self-image for the remainder of his life.

After much frustration I secured a visa to the DDR. My journey was to take the form of a perfect triangle between Altenburg, my birthplace; Leipzig, the city of my schooling; and Buchenwald Concentration Camp, the place of most of my family's death. It was there that my father had been interned for a part of 1938 and 1939. By choosing to return to this place from whence I had escaped as a child, I was heeding the alchemist's vessel where slime might be transmuted into gold. I hoped that if I was able to reevaluate my fears of old anger I could achieve balance in my life. My father's acceptance of his role as a victim was his torment and he could not help but turn his torment against those he loved, becoming a kind of criminal in his assertion of the only power he had left. To go on with my own life I had to face what could have been my death and dispel the residue of the victim left in me. At the same time,

I believed that my activity at Buchenwald could somehow help my father even in death.

As the bus passed through lush woods, approaching the camp, I imagined myself the child I might have been, traveling this road to a darker destiny. Even as I was conscious of my choice in this pilgrimage, in those moments I came to identify with the fear my father had described. I clutched my bag holding my father's prayer shawl. I also carried with me a cumbersome incised rock, which a non-Jewish friend had entrusted to me to leave as a marker acknowledging our collective conscience.

I had prepared myself to face the camp as my father had described it, but it was no longer there to be confronted. Past the beautiful gates inscribed with "Work Makes Us Free" only a few buildings remained standing. Telltale depressions in the earth are all that mark the place where barracks once housed prisoners crowded like animals. Nothing seemed real. I frantically searched for some tangible evidence of what this place had been. But even the flowering earth refused to bear witness.

I had planned to recite from the "Song of Songs," the biblical love poem Kabbalists believed to reflect creation of androgyny as the spiritual wedding of the human and the divine. And so, in June of 1984, forty-five years after we had escaped Germany, I returned as the alchemist to do the work of uniting opposites in the place of the furnace. I performed the ceremony uniting my father with his divine opposite, dancing a circular dance for his wedding. The Kabbalists feel that when we die it is our wedding day. Standing on the hill overlooking the verdant valley of Weimar, I became aware of the nourishment this landscape had offered to Schiller, Goethe, and so many other gifted artists who had lived there. As the child in me stooped to pick wildflowers for my hair, the artist in me watched and recoiled, seeing those flowers as growing from a rich earth, nourished by blood. For one frightening moment I imagined the round color wheel, red and green opposing each other as complements, knowing that their union produces brown. I struggled to reconcile my horror with glimpses of an understanding of the order of the universe.

As I read the verses, wrapped in my father's German-made prayer shawl, I found myself whipping and whirling, turning circles in the air, in the hope and belief that I was cleansing the place of an evil still present. Balancing on the threshold between the dark and the light, I chased out at its source the essence of my father's victimization so that should he return in another karmic life, he will be free of the victim image. Dancing a circle at my father's wedding, crying tears of pain and joy, I felt the washing and a whitening of the alchemical process. By facing my personal shadow I left the blackness, hoping to dance into a new future where I would become adept at being a faithful threshold dancer, a rejoicing tent bearer.

Before my father's death, much of our conversation centered on family history, particularly on my father's grandfather, a pious Polish Jew, a scribe of the Torah and knowledgeable in Kabbalah. For the last eight years, much of my work has reflected the system of Kabbalah. My choice to work in this manner was unconscious. A Jungian analyst who saw my work in an exhibition pointed out the archetype. The Kabbalah is the perennial teaching of the ten divine emanations of the androgynous deity. It is diagrammed as a tree of life, which is sometimes shown as a geometric structure. I refer to this structure in my drawings. The two opposite sides, symmetrically balanced branches of the tree, male and female, good and evil, day and night; the center, or trunk is equilibrium and union. The place of the threshold dancer. This model of the tree of life is paralleled in various disciplines of human knowledge and experienced as a symbol, metaphor, Jungian archetypes, numerology, mathematics, and models in physics and biology. Ultimately, all point to the destiny of mankind.

As I reflect on my life and the mystery of my survival, on this return to Germany for the exhibition "The Androgyne," I wonder about the irony of my Jewish contribution of the androgynous Kabbalah to this exhibition. I cannot but imagine myself as the alchemist of old, dancing the threshold as I try to make gold out of base matter. As I fold and unfold my tent I hear my great-grandfather telling my father, who then told me, that the work of the Jew is to repair him or herself, and to work toward the repair of the world—to bring it back into balance.

# Notes on Contributors

## (Authors and Translators)

**Marjorie Agosin** is the Luella Lamer Slaner Professor of Latin-American Studies at Wellesley College. She has published more than twenty books of poetry, eight books of memoirs, and six books of fiction—in Spanish and English, including: *Always from Somewhere Else: My Jewish Father; Celebration of Memory: Growing up Jewish in Latin America; Uncertain Travelers: The Jewish Emigrant Experience in the Americas;* and *Dear Anne Frank*. She has won numerous awards including the Gabriela Mistral Medal of Honor (for lifetime achievement), and the United Nations Leadership Award in Human Rights.

**Edith Altman** is a Chicago-based artist. Her experience in fleeing Nazi Germany as a child exposed her to villainy and hatred. Her embrace of the teachings of the Lubavitcher Rebbe brought her back to a world of love and joy. Her multimedia installations span the spectrum: from art as social activism to mysticism and to spirituality. Altman has exhibited extensively in venues that range from international museums, New York galleries, and German schoolhouses.

**Diana Anhalt**, a freelance writer and longtime resident of Mexico City, wrote *A Gathering of Fugitives: American Political Expatriates in Mexico 1948–1965* (Archer Books, *2001*), recently released in Spanish. Her articles, poetry, and book reviews have appeared in both Mexico and the United States.

Originally from Romania, **Miriam Ben-Yoseph** received her bachelor's and master's degrees from Hebrew University of Jerusalem and her doctorate in French literature from Northwestern University. She teaches and researches in the areas of culture, gender, and work. Recently she has focused her teaching and writing on the Holocaust and on cultural homelessness and identity issues. Her work has been published in the United States and abroad. Ben-Yoseph was selected as the 2006 Carnegie Foundation for the Advancement of Teaching Illinois Professor of the Year.

**Anthony Berris** was born and educated in the UK and has lived in Israel for more than fifty years. He is a freelance translator who has translated numerous works by Israeli authors and playwrights (including Nava Semel), and for many years taught translation at an Israeli college. He is a member of Kibbutz Beit Haemek in Western Galilee.

**Janine Canan**'s translation of the poetry of Else Lasker-Schüler, *Star in My Forehead* (HolyCow!, 2000) was a Book Sense and City Lights "Pick." Canan has published ten volumes of poetry, most recently *Changing Woman* and *In the Palace of Creation: Selected Works 1969–1999*. She is also author of a book of essays, *Goddesses, Goddesses*, and a book of stories, *Journeys with Justine*. She edited several acclaimed anthologies, including *Messages from Amma* ("Best Spiritual Books 2004") and *She Rises like the Sun: Invocations of the Goddess* (Koppelman Award). Canan graduated from Stanford with distinction and from New York University School of Medicine. She is a practicing psychiatrist in Sonoma, California.

**Ellen Cassedy** is a journalist living near Washington, D.C. Her account of her daughter's Yiddish-flavored bat mitzvah appeared in *Bridges* and *Utne Reader*. She is a contributor to *Hadassah*, *The Forward*, *Jewish Telegraphic Agency*, *and Lilith*. Her translations of Yiddish fiction have appeared in the National Yiddish Book Center's *Pakn Treger* magazine and in *Beautiful as the Moon, Radiant as the Stars: Jewish Women in Yiddish Stories* (Warner Books, 2003). She is working on a book about her journey to Lithuania where, in addition to studying Yiddish, she explored how Lithuanians are engaging with the treasures and the tragedy of the Jewish past.

**Helen Degen Cohen/Halina Degenfisz**'s awards include a National Endowment for the Arts Fellowship in Poetry, First Prize in British *Stand Magazine*'s International fiction competition, several Illinois Arts Council awards, and an Indiana Writers Conference award. She is a founding editor of *RHINO* and coordinator of its adjunct, The Poetry Forum; was Artist-in-Education through the IAC and instructor for Roosevelt University. Twice featured in the *Spoon River Poetry Review*, she is also the subject of two articles: "This Dark Poland—Ethnicity in the work of Helen Degen Cohen" (*Something of My Very Own to Say: American Women Writers of Polish Descent*, Columbia University Press); and "Rootlessness and Alienation in the Poetry of Helen Degen Cohen" (*Shofar*).

**Lisa Comforty** is coauthor and coproducer of the award-winning documentary film, *The Optimists: The Story of the Rescue of the Bulgarian Jews from the Holocaust*. The 150 hours of filmed interviews conducted with survivors from several countries are archived for scholarly use in the United States Holocaust Museum, the Simon Wiesenthal Center, and other institutions dedicated to education about the Holocaust. A writer and editor, Comforty has served in these capacities for a number of publishers and universities, including Northwestern University, the University of Chicago, Houghton Mifflin, and Rand McNally. She holds a law degree from the University of Wisconsin (1980) and a bachelor's degree from the University of Chicago (1976).

**Betty Jean Craige** is University Professor of Comparative Literature and Director of the Center for Humanities and Arts at the University of Georgia. She has published books in the fields of Spanish poetry, modern literature, history of ideas, politics, ecology, and art. Her work includes five book-length translations, *Selected Poems of Antonio Machado (1978); The Poetry of Gabriel Celaya (1984); Manuel Mantero: New*

*Songs for the Ruins of Spain (1986); Poems for Josefina* by Marjorie Agosin (2004); and *Mother, Speak to Us of War/Madre, Hablanos de la Guerra,* by Marjorie Agosin (2006).

**Dina Elenbogen** is an award-winning poet and prose writer. She is the author of the poetry collection *Apples of the Earth* (Spuyten Duyvil, NY) and a memoir in manuscript, *Drawn from Water* about her work with Ethiopian immigrants in Israel. Excerpts of it have appeared in the anthology *Lost on the Map of the World: Jewish American Women's Quest for Home in Essays and Memoir, 1890–present.* Her poetry and prose have appeared in numerous literary magazines and anthologies including *Tikkun, Chicago Reader, Midstream, Calyx,* and *Prairie Schooner.* She has received several Illinois Arts Council Literary fellowships and has been nominated for a 2007 Pushcart Prize in poetry. She is the recipient of the Miriam Lindberg Israel Poetry for Peace prize. Elenbogen teaches creative writing at the University of Chicago Graham School. She lives in Evanston, Illinois with her husband and two children.

**Jyl Lynn Felman** is an author, performance artist, and currently a visiting assistant professor of Judaic Studies at the Commonwealth College at the University of Massachusetts, Amherst. Ms. Felman's memoir *Cravings,* was published in 1997 and *Hot Chicken Wings,* a collection of short stories, was a 1993 Lambda Literary Finalist. *If Only I'd Been Born A Kosher Chicken,* her autobiographical, one woman show aired nationally in 1997 on C-SPAN'S Performance Series. Ms. Felman has appeared at over twenty-five universities in Cuba, England, Canada, the United States, Australia, and the Czech Republic. She has been featured on radio and TV, including the BBC and NPR. *Never A Dull Moment: Teaching and the Art of Performance* was recently published to wide acclaim.

**Dorothy Field** is a visual artist working with handmade paper for artists' books and dry-point prints, as well as a writer. Her first volume of poetry, *Leaving the Narrow Place,* was published in 2004. She is coauthor of *Between Gardens: Observations on Gardening, Friendship* *and Disability*, and author of a children's book *In the Street of the Temple Cloth Printer*. She has lived on Vancouver Island for more than thirty years.

**S. E. Gilman** is currently a doctoral candidate in Language and Literacy Education at Penn State University. She has been writing and publishing poems, fiction, and essays since the mid-seventies.

**Farideh Dayanim Goldin** was born on January 25, 1953, in Shiraz, Iran. She earned her graduate degrees in Humanities with emphasis on Women's Studies in 1976, and MFA in Creative Writing in 1995 from Old Dominion University. Goldin's book, *Wedding Song: Memoirs of an Iranian Jewish Woman* reveals the lives of many Iranian Jewish women in the 1950s and 1960s as well as their tales of earlier generations. Much of her writing and research, in fact, focuses on Iranian women and Iranian Jewish culture. Her articles have been published in anthologies and magazines in the United States and abroad.

**Viva Hammer** was born and raised in Sydney, Australia and came to New York where she married a man raised on the Upper East Side of Manhattan (although born downtown), and they have two children, one born uptown and one downtown. Hammer is now a partner in a Washington, D.C. law firm, and has written for *The Washingtonian*, *The Forward*, *Lilith*, as well as literary reviews and anthologies.

Though born and raised in New York City, **Arlene Hisiger** has called places as diverse as Arad, Israel, and Denver, Colorado home. Having lived in Israel and several American cities, as well as traveled extensively throughout the Far East, Hisiger is enriched by her encounter with diverse populations and cultures. She is a firm believer in "doing what you love," and credits a graduate school professor of psychology's commendation of her writing style with helping her discover what she loves. Her professor's remarks served as springboard for her latest career as freelance writer. Drawing on her life experience and her keen observer's eye, she brings characteristic wit and warmth to her subject matter.

**Daniel M. Jaffe** translated *Here Comes the Messiah!* (Zephyr Press, 2000), a Russian-Israeli novel by Dina Rubina, and compiled and edited *With Signs and Wonders: An International Anthology of Jewish Fabulist Fiction* (Invisible Cities Press, 2001). His novel, *The Limits of Pleasure* (Haworth Press, 2001), was a finalist for a ForeWord Magazine Book of the Year Award. A Pushcart Prize nominee, Jaffe teaches creative writing for the UCLA Extension Writers' Program.

**Rachel Goldin Jinich** is a recent graduate of the Brandeis International Business School where she received a master's degree in finance. Prior to her studies at Brandeis, she studied Spanish Literature and Political Science at George Washington University. She was recently married and resides with her husband in Boston.

**Cha Johnston** grew up in Johannesburg, South Africa, and has a bachelor of arts degree with majors in art history and psychology. She lives in Cape Town with her seventeen-year-old daughter Bianca, her artist partner Mark and her cat Magic in the top apartment of a 150-year-old house overlooking the silhouette of Table Mountain. With a strong interest in Jungian psychology, her poetry, written from a very early age although rarely shared with the world, is characterized by deep symbology and rich imagery navigating her inner journey as a woman. She works at the University of Cape Town in the Primary Health Care Directorate.

**Dalia Kaveh** was born in Tel-Aviv in 1943. Since 1963 she has been living in Jerusalem. She attended the Hebrew University of Jerusalem and has a BSc and MSc in biology, and a PhD in science education. She worked as a lecturer of cell biology at the pre-academic school of the Hebrew University for over thirty years. She began writing poetry after the death of her parents. She published two volumes of poetry and a third one is expected soon. Several of her poems have been published in various magazines. She has three children and six grandchildren.

**Tracy Koretsky** has won numerous awards for her fiction and poetry, including many first-place citations and three Pushcart Prize nominations. Her work is widely published in literary magazines, including *Potomac Review, The Comstock Review, and Phantasmagoria*. She runs the "Best of the Best" poetry competition for Triplopia. Her second novel, *The Body of Helen*, a roman à clef inspired by Martha Graham, has been recognized by awards from the California Writers Club, the Mary Ann Pfeffinger Awards, the Maryland Writers Association, and ReadingWriters.com.

Born in the Rhineland in 1869, **Else Lasker-Schüler** migrated to Berlin in her youth, and published ten books of poetry and prose. In 1932 at age sixty-three she received Germany's prestigious Kleist Prize. Months later "the greatest lyric poet of modern Germany," as many considered her, was accosted by Nazis waving an iron bar. She ran straight to the train station, took the next train to Zurich and never returned to Germany. She traveled on to Palestine, where she died twelve years later and was buried on the Mount of Olives. Her poem "Homesick" ("Heimweh"), first published in Berlin in her 1911 collection *My Miracles (Meine Wunder)*, expresses the longing of a soul in exile.

**Barbara F. Lefcowitz** has published nine poetry collections. Her latest collection, *The Blue Train to America* appeared in January 2007. Her fiction, poetry, and essays have been published in over 500 journals. She has won writing fellowships and prizes from the National Endowment for the Arts, the National Endowment for the Humanities, the Rockefeller Foundation, and several individual journals. A native New Yorker, Lefcowitz has lived most of her life in Bethesda, Maryland. For thirty years she taught English and creative writing at several schools, including the Writer's Center in Bethesda and several teaching programs abroad. She travels widely and is also a visual artist, focusing at present on silk painting and fused glass. Among other venues, she has given readings at the Library of Congress, and the Folger as well as several colleges around the country.

**Marcelle Levy** was born in Haut, Egypt (Sohag). At age eleven she moved with her family to Cairo where she attended a Jewish school called El Sebil. She spoke Arabic and French and learned a little

Hebrew. Levy married at age twenty and has three children. Her family left Egypt after the Six Day War and HIAS helped them emigrate to the United States. They settled in Chicago where her sister and brother, who had left Egypt in 1956, were living. Levy enrolled her children at the Anshe Emet Day School where she herself has been employed since 1973.

Canadian born **Rochelle Mass** and her husband and two young daughters moved to Israel in 1973. After living in Kibbutz Beit HaShita in the Jezre'el Valley for twenty-five years, they now live in a little community crawling up the western flank of the Gilboa mountains, in the same valley where they cure and press their own olives. She has published three poetry collections, most recently *The Startled Land* (Wind River Press). *The Belmont Collection*, a novella and short fiction, is pending publication (Wind River Press). Her awards include: twice Pushcart nominee, twice shortlisted by the BBC for a radio play and short fiction; first and second prize in Reuben Rose Poetry competition. She is widely published in journals and anthologies. An interviewer for the Steven Spielberg Holocaust Archives in Jerusalem, she is a translator and editor.

**Ada Molinoff**'s grandmother, Bella Galudger Molinovich, emigrated from Lumzdagabovna, a *shtetl* in western Russia, to New York City. David—the three-year-old who came with her—became a family physician and the poet's father. Molinoff grew up on central Long Island, NY; received her education in Massachusetts and in California; and lives in Oregon, where she is a clinical psychologist. Her poems have appeared in *Fireweed: Poetry of Western Oregon*; *The Jewish Women's Literary Annual*; and *Riven Poetry Journal*'s special issue and photographic exhibit, "Oregon Coast: Visions and Perspectives." She is interested in memoir, in both poetry and prose. She is enrolled in Pacific University's MFA in Writing program.

**Angelina Muñiz-Huberman** (Hyères, 1936) has published thirty-five books and is a guest lecturer at international universities. She introduced Jewish mysticism and Converso themes in Mexican literature. Her work has been awarded with major prizes and translated into various languages. She has received considerable international attention from leading scholars. Some of her titles are: *Morada Interior; El Mercader de Tudel; Huerto Cerrado, Huerto Sellado (translated into English as Enclosed Garden; La Lengua Florida.* She is included in anthologies such as *The Oxford Book of Jewish Stories; With Signs and Wonders; The Scroll and the Cross.* Her most recent novel is: *El Sefardí Romántico.*

**Erusha Newman** (née Joseph) was born in Pune, India (Maharashtra State) in 1933. She emigrated to the United States of America in 1976. She went to an all Catholic School in Pune for her elementary and high school education. She attended the Nowrosjee Wadia College and the Tilak College of Education and earned a bachelor of science and a bachelor in education degree from the University of Pune. She was a math and science teacher and taught grades 6 to 11 in two well-established English Medium Schools. In 1982 she graduated from the School of Library Science at Case Western Reserve University, obtaining a master's in library science. She worked as a medical librarian at the University of Illinois in Chicago and Loyola University in Maywood, Illinois. She also worked as a librarian for the Environmental Protection Agency in Chicago, Illinois, until retiring in 1996.

**Sara Paretsky** revolutionized the mystery world with her fictional detective, V. I. Warshawski. In addition to her best-selling series of crime novels, Paretsky has edited three short story collections and written the memoir *Writing in an Age of Silence*. Paretsky's deep-rooted concern for social justice, the hallmark of her novels, has carried her voice beyond the world of crime fiction. As a frequent contributor to the *New York Times* and the *Guardian*, and a speaker at such places as the Library of Congress and Oxford University, she is an impassioned advocate for those on society's margins.

**Julie Parson-Nesbitt** is author of the poetry collection *Finders* (West End Press) and coeditor of *Power Lines: A Decade of Poetry From Chicago's Guild Complex* (Tia Chucha Press). Recipient of the Gwendolyn Brooks Poetry Award, her poems have been published in *Identity Lessons* (Penguin), *Stories from Where We Live* (Milkweed Editions) and other anthologies and journals. Parson-Nesbitt served as executive director of the Guild Complex literary center and currently works with Young Chicago Authors. She holds a master of Fine Arts in Creative Writing from the University of Pittsburgh.

**Eve Perkal** left Danzig, the city of her birth, on the eve of World War II for the distant shores of Shanghai, China. After the war she immigrated to the United States and has lived in the Chicago area since 1947. Since her retirement from a career in special education, she has been busy pursuing her many, varied interests, which include courses at Northwestern University's Institute for Learning in Retirement, and National-Louis University's Lifelong Learning Institute where she coordinates the course "Writing for Your Family."

**Deborah Nodler Rosen** always seeks ways to combine her love of poetry, the Jewish people, and travel. After earning a BA from Wellesley College and a JD from the University of Pennsylvania Law School she won a Fulbright to study the Supreme Court of India. She has written a biography, *Anwar el Sadat*, and numerous poems from her travels that have been published in *The Journal*, Northwestern University, *Where We Live—Illinois Poets, Jewish Women's Literary Annual, Third Coast, Out of Line, Spoon River Poetry Review, Moment, New Poetry Appreciation*, Kunming, China, and many other journals. Her poems have won first prize in Poetry Society contests in Oregon, California and Missouri. Her travel includes a trip to Kaifeng, China, to meet descendants of the Kaifeng Jews and to Kiev, Ukraine, where she became Bat Mitzvah during a Project Kesher international Jewish women's conference.

**Maria Roth**, professor of social work and clinical psychologist, is the chair of the Social Work Department at Babes-Bolyai University in Cluj, Romania. Before entering the academic field she worked fifteen years with children, as speech therapist, school psychologist, and later as a clinical psychologist in special schools, orphanages, and hospitals. She is one of the founders of the social work studies in Romania. She spent nine months as a Fulbright senior research scholar at University of North Carolina at Chapel Hill, USA, studying prevention programs in child welfare, and then returned to her home university and published several books and articles in the area of child welfare, prevention of violence in schools and families, and changes in the Romanian welfare system.

**Dina Rubina**, one of today's most prominent Russian writers, is a four-time nominee for the Russian Booker Prize and has won literary awards in France, Israel, and Uzbekistan. Her work has been translated into a dozen languages. Her most highly acclaimed novel, *Here Comes the Messiah!* has been published in English translation (Zephyr Press, 2000), as have several of her short stories. After growing up in Tashkent, Uzbekistan, Rubina moved to Moscow in 1984, and then emigrated to Israel in 1990. In the late 1990s she returned to Moscow for three years to serve as Israel's cultural liaison.

**Sara Schwarzbaum** grew up in Buenos Aires, Argentina in a multilingual home, the daughter and granddaughter of post–World War II immigrants. Her curiosity about her family's cultural background eventually led her to pursue a career in psychology. She became an immigrant herself when she moved to the United States twenty-five years ago. Schwarzbaum is now a professor in the Couple and Family Counseling program at Northeastern Illinois University in Chicago, where she trains future family counselors. She lectures frequently on clinical issues related to working with immigrants; she has a private practice where she works with couples and families in English, Spanish, and, sometimes, in Yiddish, and she is the coauthor of *Culture and Identity: Life Stories for Counselors and Therapists* (Sage, 2006) and *Dimensions of Multicultural Counseling: A Life Story Approach* (Sage, 2008).

Israeli born author **Nava Semel** has published fifteen books and four plays, for both adults and children. Her work focuses on the painful dialogue among family members of Holocaust survivors, and the search for Israeli identity. She was published in the United States, Germany, Italy, Czech Republic, Spain, Holland, China, Turkey, Poland, and Romania. Her book *Becoming Gershona* received the 1990

YA National Jewish Book Award in the United States. Nava Semel is a recipient of the Israeli Prime Minister Award for Literature (1996), and the Woman of the Year in Literature Award (Tel Aviv, 2007).

**Caroline Smadja** is a French-American writer born in North Africa. Her essays "Motherland" and "The Search to Belong," about her Jewish Tunisian roots were published in the Canadian magazine *Kinesis* and in the anthology *The Flying Camel*, respectively. Her poem "In Absentia" appeared in *California Quarterly*. Her short story "After Dark" was published in the South African magazine, *Jewish Affairs*, and the short-shorts "Healing"and "The F Word" appeared in Paris-based *Upstairs at Duroc*. She currently resides in Paris.

**Judith Ilson Taylor** is a writer, teacher, and visual artist whose work reflects her particular interest in the creative process.

**Madeline Tiger**'s most recent collection of poetry (her eighth) is *Birds of Sorrow and Joy: New and Selected Poems, 1970–2000*, Marsh Hawk Press, 2003. Her work has appeared in many journals and anthologies. She has been teaching in the NJ Writers-in-the-Schools Program since 1974, and has been a "Dodge Poet" since 1986. She won the Artist/Teacher Award of Playwrights Theatre of New Jersey in 1993. She lived in Montclair from 1963 until moving to Bloomfield in 2000. She has five children and six grandchildren, and lives under a weeping cherry tree.

**Davi Walders**'s poetry and prose have appeared in more than 200 publications including *The American Scholar, JAMA, Lilith, Lonely Planet, Travelers Tales*, and elsewhere. She developed and directs the Vital Signs Poetry Project at NIH (National Institutes of Health in Bethesda, MD), which was funded by the Witter Bynner Foundation for Poetry. Ms. Walders often writes about being raised in Texas and Oklahoma. Her father became an oil company executive after arriving at Ellis Island as a boy from the shtetl. Her mother left her beloved New York City to become a corporate wife who taught religious school in Ponca City, OK, and Houston, TX.

**Gerda Weissmann Klein** was born in Bielsko, Poland, in 1924, and now lives in Arizona. Her late husband, Kurt Klein, was a U.S. Army Lieutenant who liberated Gerda Weissmann on May 7, 1945. She has lectured throughout the country about her experience during the Holocaust and has written several books, including *All But My Life*, her autobiography, *The Hours After*, coauthored by her late husband, and *A Boring Evening at Home*. *One Survivor Remembers*, a documentary about her experiences during the Holocaust, won an Academy Award in 1996. Another film that features her story is shown regularly at the United States Holocaust Memorial Museum. She has appeared on the *Oprah Winfrey Show*, *CBS Sunday Morning*, and was featured on *60 Minutes* and *Nightline*.

**Arlene Zide** was born in 1940 in New York City. Poet, linguist, and translator, her poetry has appeared widely in journals both in the United States and India, for example, in *Rattapallax*, *Meridians*, *RHINO*, *Xanadu*, *Women's Review of Books*, *Primavera*, *Oyez Review*, *The Colorado Review*, *California Quarterly*, *The Spoon River Quarterly*, *Off Our Backs*, and in anthologies such as *In Love United*, *Kiss Me Goodnight*, and *Rough Places*. On a Fulbright to India, she collected and translated poetry for her anthology, *In Their Own Voice: The Penguin Anthology of Contemporary Indian Women Poets*, Penguin (India), 1993; and her translations, mostly from Hindi, appear widely in journals such as *Paintbrush*, *Salt Hill*, *The Malahat Review*, *Smartish Pace*, *Chicago Review*, *Oxford Anthology of Indian Poets*, and *The Bitter Oleander*.

**Linda Stern Zisquit** is poetry editor for *Maggid*. She has published three full-length collections of poetry: *Ritual Bath* (1993), *Unopened Letters* (1996), and *The Face in the Window* (2004), as well as a number of books of translations from Hebrew, including *Let the Words: Selected Poems* of Yona Wallach (Sheep Meadow, 2006). She has lived in Israel since 1978 with her husband and five children. She teaches at Bar Ilan University, and runs ARTSPACE, an art gallery in Jerusalem representing contemporary Israeli artists. She was awarded a writer's grant from the Memorial Foundation for Jewish Culture for

2005–2006 to complete a new collection of poems, *Porous*. She has also completed a collection of translations from the work of Israeli poet Rivka Miriam.